TEMPTATIONS FAMILIES FACE

Breaking Patterns That Keep Us Apart

Tom L. Eisenman

InterVarsity Press
Downers Grove, Illinois

InterVarsity Press® is the book-publishing division of InterVarsity Christian Fellowship®, a student movement active on campus at hundreds of universities, colleges and schools of nursing in the United States of America, and a member movement of the International Fellowship of Evangelical Students. For information about local and regional activities, write Public Relations Dept., InterVarsity Christian Fellowship, 6400 Schroeder Rd., P.O. Box 7895, Madison, WI 53707-7895.

All Scripture quotations, unless otherwise indicated, are taken from the HOLY BIBLE, NEW INTERNATIONAL VERSION®. NIV®. Copyright © 1973, 1978, 1984 by International Bible Society. Used by permission of Zondervan Publishing House. All rights reserved.

Cover photograph: Dale Durfee/Tony Stone Images
ISBN 0-8308-1688-7

Printed in the United States of America ∞

Library of Congress Cataloging-in-Publication Data

Eisenman, Tom.
   Temptations families face: breaking patterns that keep us apart/
Tom L. Eisenman.
     p.   cm.
   Includes bibliographical references.
   ISBN 0-8308-1688-7 (cloth: alk. paper)
   1. Family—United States. 2. Family—Religious life. 3. Conduct
of life. I. Title.
HQ536.E39   1996
306.85—dc20   95-48957
                                            CIP

17	16	15	14	13	12	11	10	9	8	7	6	5	4	3	2	1
10	09	08	07	06	05	04	03	02	01	00	99	98	97	96		

We dedicate this book to
Jana, Joshua, Jason and Gabriel,
with all our respect and love,
and to all families like our own
who struggle each day to find new ways
to know and love each other more deeply.

1

Tempted
to Let Life's Rush
Swallow Us Up

•

The rush of life today is sweeping our families along and eating us alive. We are spinning out of control. The centrifugal force of life in the fast lane has thrust the primary needs of healthy families to the periphery, while a rush of secondary concerns has gravitated to the core. Being loved and sharing love are the essence of what makes family life work. But living in love requires time and energy, commodities that are in short supply in fast-track families.

What we need most today is to recover in our families the meaningful community experience the Bible describes as *koinōnia*. This rich biblical word, taken from the Greek root *koin,* means essentially "to share." Koinonia in the family is sharing life together at the most intimate levels. It is participating in each other's lives in a wholesome and nurturing way, learning to support and care for one another. It is also learning to trust so that we can feel safe enough in our families to be truly open, honest and real with one another.

The family provides a wealth of opportunities to explore what it means to love. Jack and Judith Balswick describe what we hope for in our families when they write:

In the intimacy of the family community, we have a place where we can be naked and not ashamed (Gen. 2:25), a place where we can be who we are, free from all the demanding requirements of the outside world. Here is a place where family members can relax and be comfortable in a supportive and encouraging atmosphere. Here they do not have to hide, but can be honest and real before the others in the family.[1]

To build our families toward this ideal takes time and focused energy. To be a family in more than name only, we need more than anything else a generous amount of quality relational time. We need to find a less frantic and more relaxed pace if we are to experience family life as it was meant to be. It takes relaxed time to really get to know one another, to share in each other's struggles and dreams and to simply enjoy being a family.

Merely spending time together does not guarantee quality family interaction. Skills for family living still have to be acquired. But if we fail to guard time for relationship in our families, opportunities to give and receive love are simply swallowed up in frantic activity. If we give our best time to the demands of life in the fast lane, our families get what's left over—time crumbs.

Breaking the Cycle

It was a number of years ago that I first had to face the fact that I was allowing myself to be swallowed up in the rush and drive of pastoral work. I was a young man on my way up in a large and exciting church. I was beginning to be recognized, sought after. I was making a difference everywhere I went. My attention was subtly shifting away from my family priorities and toward the increasing demands and rewards of ministry. My spending long hours at work, or traveling, or away from home in the evenings was hurting Judie and the children, but I did not see it.

I finally came to my senses while preparing for a talk to preschool fathers. My topic was the importance of spending quality time with our young children. In preparation for the talk I looked over my ministry calendar for the previous five weeks. Of the thirty-six evenings available in that time span, I had been home only eight nights. There were six Sunday nights in that stretch of time, and I had been home with my family on just two of them.

I began my talk that night to the large gathering of young fathers by saying, "I'm here tonight because I need help with a major problem I have as a father. I'll give you a picture of my problem." I put my calendar on the overhead projector and then opened things up for discussion. I said, "I hope you can help straighten me out, for my sake and for the sake of my family." Those fathers were very helpful to me and to each other in discussing the reasons for overscheduling and spending too much time away from our families. I learned a lot about myself that night and walked away determined to grow in this area.

That evening with the preschool fathers opened my eyes to some less-than-spiritual motivations for ministry. My ministry looked like sacrificial service, but in reality I was driven by an unhealthy need for public affirmation. Being affirmed in my work was more powerful for me than it should have been. Once I took a closer look at why I was making such bad choices, Judie and I could begin to make the changes necessary for me to become the husband and father I really wanted to be. Acknowledging the unhealthy motives behind my rush of activity gave me the will to change. I gave myself permission to start saying no—to break the self-destructive pattern that was making me a stranger to my own children.

The first thing I did was tell the church staff at a meeting later that week that I was taking on a new life goal—*planned irresponsibility*. I told them that I needed to make a dramatic change in the way I approached my work in ministry. If I didn't change, I would be putting my health in jeopardy and, more important, risk losing the family I loved.

The staff was very supportive. Most of my friends on staff had previously encouraged me to take more time for my family. They

[11]

had always thought I was overly conscientious and perfectionistic about my work. They were surprised to hear me confess the discoveries I was making about my unhealthy ego needs and mixed motivations for ministry.

The next thing I did was work with Judie on scheduling. We blocked out weekend family time that could not be compromised and set an absolute standard for the number of nights I could be away from our family in a month. The very next evening I went over a committee agenda by phone with the chairperson and told him I could not be at the meeting that night. The children heard me say for the first time in a long time, "I want to be home with my family."

That following Saturday was a great day. I took our three little boys across the road from our house. There we found a gully where farm families must have dumped all their junk years ago. For an hour or more we dug and sifted through the dirt. We were junior archaeologists, digging up forgotten treasures of times gone by: bottles with ancient dates on them, funny-looking old shoes, scraps of magazines with pictures and advertisements from generations past. After that we spotted a bird's nest way up in a tree. The boys were afraid to climb up, so I went. They all fell to the ground laughing when I got snagged on a branch that pulled my pants down, leaving my bare backside sticking out of my jeans. Later we heard some shooting, so we had to keep our heads down, hiding and crawling on our hands and knees down the gully like soldiers, peeking carefully up over the bank. We found some really neat rocks. We saw a hang glider. There was a long, hard hill to climb, and Gabe made it. We all told him we were proud.

We sat in an abandoned shack to have our lunch. It was fun to imagine who might have lived there, how long ago, and what their life was like. There was an old, broken-down horse cart outside that we climbed on. We hiked over to an oil derrick and talked about how it worked. On the way home we picked grasses and flowers for Mom.

[12]

It was one of the great days of my life, and memorable for the boys as well. It cost me nothing. I just took time to be with my kids.

I could not help but play through my mind some family conversations from a couple of weeks previous. On my way out one night, our first-grade daughter, Jana, said to me, "Dad, I know what Christianity is now."

I stopped. I was excited to hear. She continued, "It's a lot of meetings in your life."

That week my son Jason had come to me with the same question every night. He would say, "Dad, are you going to be home tonight?" My answers were "No," "No," "No," "No," "No" and finally "Yes."

"Oh, good," he said that last time. He was so happy that I could find one night to be with him in six days.

I also remembered a conversation with Judie. She said, "You're going to have to do something about this."

I said, "That's all I need. As hard as this time is for me, I don't need *you* on my back besides. Why do you think I'm doing this? It's for us, for the kids." She just looked at me.

My failures in this area have made me very sensitive to how easy it is to live in denial, to become addicted to excitement, to the feeling that if we are busy we must be worth something. We can convince ourselves of the rightness of our rushed lifestyles, even though we often feel stressed out, pressured and overwhelmed. We find it difficult to believe that our lifestyle might be contributing to our family's problems.

So often now in family counseling, parents tell me with an obvious sense of pride about their demanding work schedules, their numerous new projects or investments, their busy social calendars, their involvement in community concerns and their exciting church activities. The only problems they recognize involve their children. If they could only get these irritating little snags with their kids worked out (little things like their teenager's alcohol and drug addiction, trouble with police over shoplifting and vandalism, sexual promiscuity, the younger daughter's violent outbursts at school and in the home), everything would be just fine. It seems increasingly difficult to help parents see that their lifestyle choices contribute to their family problems. And if they can see it, finding ways to break out of the complex patterns and move toward greater health, balance and sanity in family life is even harder.

We are powerfully tempted today to sacrifice family life to what the world offers our egos through career incentives, accumulated commodities and self-improvement programs. Many of us have allowed ourselves to be swept too far downstream in a current of secular values and attitudes that tears the fragile fabric of family life. It's easy to live in denial. I know this all too well from personal experience. When challenged we will often try to defend our crazy lifestyles. Our children cry for attention, but their cries fall on deaf ears. We tell them we are doing it all for them, for their sake, their happiness, for the good of the family. Temptations to virtue are always the most difficult to recognize and resist.

To Have It All
One popular idea that contributes to the fast pace of contemporary life is that having more money and possessions will somehow make us happy. It is difficult to resist today's constant media assault, which hammers into our heads the idea that happiness is the natural result of acquiring an abundance of things. Advertising has just two basic messages: you do not yet have everything you need, and what you already have is not good enough (a newer model has just come out). We seem to be captivated by the idea that having that new thing, or the latest model of the old thing, will suddenly bring the happiness we seek.

If we believe this is true for ourselves, we will also believe it is true for our kids. We will want them to have everything so that they will be happy too. This line of thinking is terribly misguided and throws us head over heels into the fast-track lifestyle.

We feel the pressure to acquire more things to appear successful and achieve happiness. If we can't afford what we think we need, we charge it. We can inflate our standard of living by combining credit with income. Credit is easy to obtain but very difficult to control. We become accustomed to living above our means, convincing ourselves that we can't live without the things we have. But now added to the pressure of acquiring more to maintain happiness is the stress and anxiety of growing debt. We have to work harder (and usually longer and longer hours) to try to keep up. If there are two parents in the family, both will be working longer and harder to meet the obligations required by the ballooning family debt.

In Ecclesiastes, Solomon writes, "Whoever loves money never has money enough; whoever loves wealth is never satisfied with his income" (Eccles 5:10). If we love money and the inanimate objects money can buy, we are emotional necrophiliacs. We love dead things. We need to love our families—not money, not things. Are you susceptible to the message that happiness is having more and more? Are you tempted to defend your drivenness by claiming you do it all for the family?

My friend Paul told me he was doing it all for his family. Paul worked for the largest bakery firm in the world. He was an executive on the way up, fast. It was a critical season in his career. During one five-year period he moved his family seven times. Each move brought Paul a higher salary, greater prestige, more power and acclaim. And each move also brought more of the things he felt would make his family happy—nicer cars, bigger and more attractive homes and an abundance of life's accessories.

The seventh move was to Milwaukee, Wisconsin. The family arrived on Monday and met the moving van outside their new home. Tuesday morning Paul immersed himself in his new job. That Thursday at noon he was called home from work. A service man heard the family car running in the garage and called police. The garage was thick with exhaust and fumes. Paul's wife had committed suicide. She was dead in the front seat of the car.

Paul told me he had been getting messages from every direction, but he had refused to listen. He was a man on a mission. And it cost him the most important thing in life to himself and his four children. Paul found out too late that the price for his drivenness was too high.

After his wife committed suicide, Paul refused further promotions. He spent more time with his family. After five years he married again, quit his work as an executive and dedicated his life to leading marriage enrichment seminars. Now he devotes himself to preventing young men and women from making the same mistakes he made.

Paul learned the hard way that some things are worthless pursuits. Like a desert mirage, they promise fulfillment, but they don't deliver. You can pour the best years of your life into something and come up empty.

To Be the Perfect Parent

Michelle enjoys a reputation as a loving and caring person, a model servant in her church and community. Her husband, Bob, has a good job and a substantial salary, which gives Michelle the freedom to spend her time in volunteer work. As a member of her church deacon board, Michelle loves to help out whenever individual needs or family crises arise. She is also a dedicated Sunday-school teacher and has not taken time off from that church commitment for ten years.

Michelle is on the homeowners' association board and personally welcomes all newcomers to her area. But most important to her, she is very involved in her son and daughter's school functions. She has a gift for organizing special events and is often the first one called when something needs to be planned. Michelle likes being known as someone dependable who will do a top-notch job. For the last three years she has organized all the fundraising events for her kids' sports programs.

The crisis came for Michelle and Bob when their daughter Kelly became pregnant in her junior year of high school. It was the last thing Michelle ever thought she would have to deal with as a Christian mom with a good Christian family. During intensive family counseling Kelly was finally able to tell her parents how lonely she had always been in their family. She felt they never really cared very much about her. Dad was always at work or traveling, and Mom was always out helping other people or on the phone organizing some event.

Astonished and in tears, Michelle said to Kelly, "But honey, I was your leader in Girl Scouts and your Sunday-school teacher, and I was there for you every time your softball team needed someone to do a fundraiser or to have all the kids over for the team get-togethers."

Kelly said, "Mom, you did things *for* me, but you never do anything *with* me. I feel like I'm invisible to you and Dad. I feel like everybody else outside the family has always been more important to you than I am." Kelly finally got her parents' attention.

Michelle was known as a supermom to everyone around her at church, at school and throughout the community. It turned out that neither Kelly nor Michelle's son Rob felt that she was a supermom *to them*. The rush of Michelle's life and her commitment to activities outside the home swallowed up all the available time she could and should have spent developing loving and intimate relationships with her children.

Like so many others I've counseled, Michelle had grown up in a home where she was affirmed only when she performed well. Somewhere along the way she mixed up who she *was* with what she *did*. Even as an adult, she felt she had to prove her worth each and every day. The fact that she did not have a career fueled her feelings of insecurity. Michelle felt she had to say yes to every challenge or request that came her way. And she felt she needed to accomplish each task at the very highest level of competence. It was through doing good works, being seen by others as a selfless servant, that Michelle built her self-esteem.

If we believe consciously or subconsciously that our worth is determined by how much we achieve and how well we accomplish what we do, we will set very high goals for ourselves and try our hardest to meet them. If we are perfectionistic to boot, we will always feel that we could do more or do it better. So the next time we take on a project or activity, we shoot higher. We find each new level of perfection harder to reach. So we fall short of our expectations again and again. Each time our self-esteem takes a hit. The perfectionistic personality cannot judge personal performance without automatically making a judgment on personal self-worth. You are what you do. This is a self-defeating downward spiral that generates trying harder and harder, under intense stress from fear of failure. It is a perfect recipe for drowning in a rush of activity.

Unless we can learn to adjust our expectations, accept our limitations and still feel good about ourselves, we will find it impossible to balance our lifestyle. The rush of doing more and more but feeling like we are accomplishing less and less will destroy us. If we are out of control in this area, we will become missing persons in our families. There will be no family time. This is the trap Michelle was in. She depleted herself on secondary loyalties. There was no time or emotional strength to meet the deepest needs of her children, who wanted nothing more than a loving relationship with their mom.

To Fulfill Ourselves

The quest for self-fulfillment has also kept us running. Many today seem to fear missing out on anything good. They buy into the "you only go around once, so go for all the gusto you can get" attitude. I remember reading about Dr. Robert Arnot in *Sports Illustrated* and thinking how he epitomized the self-fulfillment lifestyle. The article reported that he "sleeps three hours a night to have time to board sail, speed skate, run, bicycle, doctor, dance, romance, and play the trumpet."[2] Those who fall into this trap seem to be trying to suspend the movement of time by speeding up the pace of everything they do.

We are led to believe that we will find ultimate happiness and fulfillment through a process of continual self-discovery and self-satisfaction. Some act as if it is a crime to harbor any unfulfilled need. They view personality as a kind of ice-cube tray and life as an ongoing adventure aimed at discovering how to fill every empty slot to the brim.

This "duty-to-self" ethic fuels a myriad of modern pursuits that can turn into life-gobbling obsessions: bodybuilding, diet and exercise, entrepreneurial adventures, playing with marriage, social climbing, the pursuit of status or prestige. It is a sign of our times that so many young couples choose to remain childless solely to pursue their individual lives unhindered. One young man, Steve, put it this way. "Why have children? Neither April nor I particularly like kids, and if we had them, think of all we would have to give up—leisurely nights alone, frequent meals out, new cars, vacations abroad."[3]

Carl Thoreson, who worked with a team at Stanford to study the effects of fast-paced living on family life, believes the most dangerous attitude of parents today is what he calls "a kind of rugged individualism gone berserk. Too many parents seem intent on 'doing their own thing,' striving to get ahead socially and economically. They believe it's enough for them to give things to their children rather than time and affection, the kind of caring and sharing that allows the child to grow up feeling good about who he is."[4] It is not surprising that the "me generation" has had such a difficult time sustaining success in marriage and is at a loss to know what has happened to the kids. You simply cannot be radically committed to self-interest and also expect to experience meaningful family lives marked by responsible love.

When couples get married or have children purely out of self-interest, they set themselves up for certain failure. Good marriages are fun, and there is pleasure in raising children. But these blessings are always the result of long-term commitment and a significant investment of time and energy focused on the family. Parents who seek primary fulfillment through their careers can lose this perspective and begin to see their children as a hindrance to finding themselves, to attaining their personal goals.

A therapist involved with the Stanford study told of an eight-year-old girl whose level of anxiety was so great that she was tearing her hair out in clumps. The parents who brought her to him said, "Fix her so we can get on with our lives." The little girl came home every day to an empty house. She lived with the daily stress of not knowing whether one or both of her parents would be home or gone on a business trip, or whether anyone would tuck her in at night. The therapist asked the little girl to describe how she felt. She said, "Like there's a hole in my heart."[5]

Sylvia Ann Hewlett speaks of these changes in terms of a cultural shift in the "giving-getting compact" that affects how parents view and treat children in our families today. In the fifties the compact for parents would have leaned heavily toward giving rather than getting. But now any notion of sacrifice—costly giving without concern for getting a fair share back—flies in the face of the values that have captured our culture. Hewlett says, "The current getting-giving compact reads as follows: I give time, energy, resources to a relationship as long as my needs are being fulfilled, as long as I am being stroked. If I become unhappy (or just plain bored), I have every right to move on to seek what I need elsewhere."[6]

When parents are absorbed in their own worlds and with their own needs, children suffer. There is simply no way to have personal freedom and fulfillment of every desire and at the same time raise healthy children. Unfortunately, many parents make choices today without regard to how the choices will affect their children's lives.

For several decades the American economy supported the self-fulfillment ideology. The economic picture was marked by dynamic, rapid growth and expanding opportunities. Ever-increasing levels of material well-being were accepted as the ongoing standard for American life. In recent years, growth has decelerated. Stocks plummeted. The bottom dropped out of the real estate market. Oil went from boom to bust. The cost of living soared, gobbling up disposable income. Unemployment skyrocketed. Savings have been depleted in many families who now struggle just to fund the basics.

These changes have tarnished the self-fulfillment mystique. Jobs are now taken rather than chosen. Many cannot even get work in the field of their training and interest. Fewer still find that perfect job which provides for creativity and enjoyment, an abundance of time off and a steadily increasing salary and benefit package to fund self-development diversions. Many baby boomers and baby busters now face a different kind of reality. This splash of cold water in the face is good if it helps us finally recognize that the pursuit of happiness through self-fulfillment is built on a very fragile foundation.

There is no way to experience it all and still have time to devote to family life. We have to learn what parts of the whole warrant our time and commitment. Then we need the strength and courage to live out our convictions. Trying to *have it all* will only keep us gasping for air as we frantically tread water in the rushing rapids of our fast-paced lives. It is simply impossible to beat time by picking up the pace. There is no way to suspend time by trying to stuff two or three lifetimes into one. We will only kill ourselves trying, and leave our hurting and confused kids in the wake. We need to make better family-oriented decisions with the limited amount of time we have.

Getting Our Heads Above Water

The rush of modern life has simply caught a lot of families off guard. Even if our intentions are good, it is hard to stop the flow of activity long enough to catch our breath and consider what needs to be changed and how we might go about changing it.

A typical day for Cathy pictures this survival mode that is common for so many families today. Cathy was up at 5:30 a.m. She set out breakfast for her family, got herself ready for work, left her home in New Jersey and took two buses for her two-hour commute to work. Cathy had hardly taken off her coat in the office at a New York City hospital cardiology unit before the rush hit—telephone, patients, surgeons clamoring for her attention. At around 10:30 a.m. she was standing with the phone cradled on her shoulder and simultaneously trying to deal with a patient waiting to talk, a colleague with a question about another patient's chart, a buzzing intercom line, two lighted buttons on her telephone indicating incoming calls, and her boss, who emerged from his office with a sheet of paper, saying, "Cathy, I need this copied right away, please." This was a fairly normal work pace for Cathy each and every day, throughout the day. But at the end of the workday, nothing slowed down for her.

At 5:00 p.m. Cathy left work, took the two-hour bus trip home again, got in her car and rushed to pick up her ten-year-old, Candra, from ballet school. Finally home, she got on the phone to work out a problem with a missed appointment and to arrange a weekend car pool. After that she helped her husband pack for a trip, tested her son Andre for a quiz he was taking the next day and then started supper for the family. During conversation at dinner the frantic family pace began to take its toll. There was an angry explosion between Candra and her father. It ended up badly, without reconciliation, but there was little time for Cathy to help work things out. There were dishes to do, and everything had to be prepared for the morning rush.[7]

Everyone in this family was drowning in a torrent of activity. No one could stop long enough to consider how things might be managed better. Cathy was suffering most from the intensity and stress of her daily schedule, but some of this could be alleviated with help from the rest of the family. Cathy's husband could pick up many of the after-work tasks, such as getting Candra home from ballet and helping Andre with his homework. The kids could be more involved in the work at home after school, helping prepare supper and cleaning up afterward. Much of what needed to be done at home could be done by the time Cathy came home. Division of labor in the home could slow down the rush of life for this family and create some family time for more healthy interaction. A good rule in this home would be "No one sits down until everyone sits down."

It is still the case in too many families that Mom does most of the shopping, cooking, housework and general parenting. Eighty percent of mothers are now in the work force either full or part time—a major cultural change that has added to family stress.[8] I will talk more about the effects of these developments in a later chapter for mothers.

Swimming Upstream in a Downstream World

All of us who care deeply about family life must resolve to "keep [ourselves] from being polluted by the world" (Jas 1:27). If the family is our highest priority, we need to do the tough work of bringing our lifestyle choices in line with our priorities.

Perhaps your family is caught up in the more-is-better mindset, and you are exhausting yourselves by trying to have it all. If so, then you have work to do. What is behind your desire to accumulate wealth and things and to be seen by others as successful? Do you feel like you have to prove something to someone? Do you feel pressure from your parents or in-laws to be something more? Is it peer pressure that drives you? Are you drowning in debt? Do you work longer and longer hours to acquire more of the things you really don't need? Do you take every promotion offered in order to keep climbing the ladder of wealth and prestige?

If you want quality family life, you will have to come to grips with these issues. What can you begin to do today that would eventually change your lifestyle and free you to have more time and energy to devote to each other in your family?

I'll never forget the courageous decision one of my friends made. He was offered a job promotion at twice his current salary. After thoroughly considering the generous offer, he turned it down. The manager came to talk with him again. He asked if my friend understood that the new job would pay him twice the salary he was currently getting. Yes, he understood that, but he also saw that the job would require twice as much travel at a time when his teenage daughter and son were both struggling with issues that required having Dad at home. The huge increase in pay was a temptation, but he was not willing to trade precious family time for more money, possessions or prestige.

We have to be honest with ourselves. If the rush of our lives leaves family time in the dust, we need to find out what's driving us. If you know that you spend far too much time wrapped up in your work, admit this to yourself. Try to uncover the source of the obsession. You may need to talk with someone who understands this aspect of your personality and can help you overcome these destructive patterns.

If you know that you live for yourself to the detriment of your family, be honest. If you see your particular obsession as an asset, a good quality that is really a blessing to others, stop and listen to your family. Hear what their real needs are, what they need from you as a husband or father, as a wife or mother. Quit defending yourself and start listening with your heart. Ask God to help you see yourself clearly. Ask him to deliver you from the distractions that drain away time and energy from your marriage and family.

When the Way Out Isn't Clear

Today many families, especially single-parent families, struggle to escape the frenzy, but the way out isn't easy or clear. Even if the single parent has a deep commitment to family values, the circumstances of life make it nearly impossible to find the time to nurture

[24]

healthy family interaction. The church today can focus more energy and resources toward helping these struggling families secure precious time for parenting the children of our future.

In the California mountain community where Judie and I now live, most families heat their homes with wood because of the high cost of propane and electricity. The church here has a program called the Do Wooders. Last year they delivered seventy-five cords of free firewood to struggling families in our community. I was gratified to learn that 47 percent of this wood was given to single-parent moms, and 80 percent of these moms were not members of the church. When the Do Wooders deliver wood, they ask these single-parent moms about their family needs. These moms often receive help with food, plumbing and electrical problems, cleaning, maintenance and even emergency child care. The church is committed to helping single moms with these expensive and time-consuming household problems in the hope that they can capture a few more precious moments with their children.

The church is an excellent network for helping single parents improve their life situation, whether it's finding better-paying jobs, offering practical counsel, teaching repair skills or providing them a respite from stress. Churches need to include single parents in the planning of family activities. Exhausted single parents feel guilty about the lack of time with their kids, but they don't know where to turn for help. The church can minister to that need. Men in the church can consider how they might become surrogate fathers or grandfathers to young children whose families have been abandoned by their fathers.

We can also become more intentional in supporting other families who are under stress, so that struggling parents can still devote priority time to their families. I remember a period in the early years of my ministry when we had a daughter in first grade and three sons of preschool age and were struggling desperately to make ends meet. With three toddlers, Judie was not able to work. It seemed to us that there were no good choices for improving our financial situation without significantly sacrificing our desire to keep family time at a high priority. A group of men at the church had put together a tax-free fund aimed at helping young families who were in a financial bind like we were. It always seemed that at the most critical time they would send us a check for $350 or $500. I have no idea what we would have done without that money. We might have been forced out of our home and into a rental. That extra money kept us afloat until our situation improved.

The Cost of Losing Perspective

A few years ago, the community we lived in was shocked when two prominent oil-company executives died in the crash of a small plane. Friends and associates stood up at the funeral of one of the men to talk about how amazing he was, how committed he was to excellence, how much he had accomplished for the company in his brief life. They held him up as a model member of the community.

After a long procession of admirers delivered a steady stream of accolades, one of the man's teenage boys stood up and walked to the microphone. He said he wished he had something good to say about his dad, but he didn't. With tears in his eyes and his voice cracking, he said he wished he knew the man these people talked so highly about—his dad. But he never knew him.

This effective executive who had apparently accomplished so much in the corporation to which he devoted his life was a virtual stranger to his own children. What does it profit us to gain the whole world if we lose the families we love?

Questions for Discussion

1. In what ways is the rush of life today eating up your family time?

2. If you had more family time, how would you put it to good use?

3. The author identifies four factors that commonly contribute to fast-paced living:

a. the indiscriminate pursuit of money and material things (the "more is better" mindset)

b. the need to prove by our perfect performance that we are worth something (perfectionism)

c. the drive for self-fulfillment at almost any cost

d. poor family management (inability to control the rush of meaningless activity)

Share with your spouse or group which of these factors tempt you to lose your family focus.

4. The author quotes Sylvia Ann Hewlett on the changes that have occurred in the "giving-getting compact" (see page 20). Do you agree that parents today seem less willing than parents of generations past to sacrifice personal needs for the good of their families? Give examples from your experience to support your answer.

5. If the rush of life is swallowing up time that you would like to devote to building family health and closeness, what are you going to do about it?

2
Tempted to
Be an Absentee
Father

•

Last year I spoke on fathers and fathering to a large group of men at the Forest Home Conference Center in southern California. After the evening session, a young man in his mid-twenties came up to talk. Tim recounted his painful memories of growing up in a home where his father was physically present but emotionally aloof and distant. He could not ever remember having a meaningful conversation with his dad. Throughout Tim's entire childhood his dad only showed up at one activity in which Tim was involved.

My son Gabe was along with me for the weekend. He stood near Tim and me, listening to the young man's story. Gabe and I were having such a great time together in a beautiful cabin, playing cards and games, sitting in front of the fire together and talking late each night.

The only thing Tim's dad showed up for was one of his son's Little League baseball games. He took pictures while he was there. When he got them developed, he brought them to his boy with a sense of pride, saying, "I took some pictures of you at the game last week."

Tim looked at them. He said, "Dad. That's not me. That's Scotty!" Tim's dad was not familiar enough with the way his son looked in his baseball uniform to take pictures of the right boy at bat.

At that point in the story I saw the hurt well up in Tim's eyes. I said, "Can I give you a hug?" Without waiting for an answer, I grabbed hold of him and just held him. He put his head down on my shoulder and sobbed in my arms. For a moment I know I became a surrogate dad for Tim. When I let him go, I glanced over at Gabe. His eyes were full of tears.

The Fathering Crisis

This kind of shame and pain is prevalent in a whole generation of young men and women. In my estimation, we are in a fathering crisis in our land. And things do not appear to be getting better. Not yet, anyway.

The largest percentage of adult men and women I see in counseling struggle with the pain of damaged or nonexistent relationships with their fathers. These men and women become locked in at a certain stage of emotional development and can't move on. They are still trying to gain the love and affirmation they need and long for from their fathers. It is the consuming passion of their lives.

It is as if the prophecy in Malachi 4:5-6 has come true in our day. The warning of the Lord is spoken this way: "See, I will send you the prophet Elijah before that great and dreadful day of the LORD comes. He will turn the hearts of the fathers to their children, and the hearts of the children to their fathers; or else I will come and strike the land with a curse."

We need to regain lost ground in fathering, to establish again a vision for the significance of fathering and to heal the hearts of young men who have not been fathered well. We need to do all we can to help young men today to become strong fathers—men broken in love with compassion for their own father-hungry children. It is the presence of strong and loving fathers in sufficient numbers that will, in the coming years, determine whether our

[29]

currently fragile society will stand or fall.

Where have all the fathers gone? The sheer load of stress related to work and long commutes has created a father vacuum in thousands of homes. Fathers get up early and leave for work before their children are even out of bed. And they don't return home until after dinnertime, when their children are getting ready for bed. These fathers can go for days without sharing meaningful time with their sons and daughters. And even if they do get some time at night, dads are often so worn out that they may be physically present but not alert or energetic enough to enter into family life on an authentic emotional level.

Former North Carolina State basketball coach Jim Valvano, whose team won a national championship against Houston in 1983, recently died of cancer at the age of forty-seven. In a touching final interview with *Sports Illustrated* Valvano spoke about the effect of his drivenness on his family. He said,

I remember one Father's Day when I happened to be home, and nobody had planned anything, nobody even mentioned it. How could they have planned anything? I'd probably never been home on Father's Day before. I might've been in Atlanta giving a Father's Day speech or in Chicago receiving a Father of the Year award, but you can bet I wasn't at home on Father's Day. Finally I asked them what we were going to do, and my daughter Jamie said, "Dad, we spent all our lives being part of your life. When are you going to be part of *ours?*" It hit me like a punch in the stomach.[1]

Divorce has also contributed to the absence of fathers from the home. The epidemic divorce rate in Western nations has left a multitude of single moms to shoulder the responsibility of caring for their children alone. A chilling study recently noted that half of all fathers fail to see their children again after a divorce.[2] Even fathers who have the best intentions will struggle to find adequate time for fathering in a shared custody situation. Job-related moves that come in the wake of a divorce only intensify the distance between fathers and their children.

Increasing numbers of father-deprived sons are not effective fathers themselves. They also add to the fathering crisis. These fathers, too, may be physically present in their homes, but they are not good fathers. They don't know how to father, because they have not had a good father model—good teaching, training, loving. This was Tim's major concern as he continued to talk with me that weekend at Forest Home. As much as he hated experiencing his father's inability to communicate with him, Tim saw that he too struggled to know how to communicate well and be involved with his own children.

The essential roles of the effective father are to be involved with his children rather than aloof, to be a strong family leader in a healthy, loving manner and to show his children how to affectionately sustain a meaningful long-term commitment to one woman—the children's mother—in marriage. But if a son has not experienced these realities, he will be ill-equipped to be a strong and loving father for his children.

A son whose masculinity is not affirmed by a loving father or strong father substitute will struggle to find himself and will often fail in his fathering because he lacks the inner security that leads to emotional health. If a man is not secure in himself, he cannot pass on a sense of security to his sons and daughters. Leanne Payne captures the essence and significance of the problem well when she says,

> Men who are unable to fully accept themselves lose to one degree or another the power to act as father, husband, and leader. In short, in at least some part of their personalities they remain immature and become increasingly passive and unable creatively to initiate the changes needed to lift themselves and their families out of the inevitable quagmires of life. The power is within them to do so. The masculine qualities and gifts are there, but they have not been "affirmed" into life.[3]

As a result, millions of fathers today act out their insecurity as

[31]

passive, immature, macho or obsessively perfectionistic men. Family members may call these men "Father," but they are not good fathers. We should not be surprised at the violence in our homes and on the streets, at young people who turn to drugs and alcohol to escape the pain of their brokenness, at confused young men who try to obtain the masculinity they long for by engaging in sexual relationships with other men, and at the young people who commit suicide to kill the fathers who live within them, the fathers they hate.

A whole and secure man, living comfortably in his masculine identity, can pass on a healthy sense of masculinity to his sons and affirm the femininity of his daughters. He can creatively influence and enhance the quality of family life. But if we have not been affirmed by this kind of father, it will be difficult for us to rest securely in our individuality as men or as women.

What's So Important About a Dad?

Fathers make a significant impact from the very beginning of a child's life. Those who are actively and lovingly involved with their kids powerfully influence the development of healthy individuals.

A baby in the womb has no sense of individuality, of separation from its mother. At birth a child experiences the intense trauma of physical separation, but its psychological sense of identity has not changed. The infant now lives outside the mother, but experiences life as if the umbilical cord had never been cut.

This bond between mother and child is one of the most powerful of human ties. The positive significance of this loving bond will be developed later in the chapter on mothers. But very early, children must begin the crucial developmental task of growing away from this strong bond with their mother, until they finally achieve full and healthy separation from her as individual adults. Whole and healthy adulthood for any child will result only after a long and difficult journey toward successful separation from Mother. The father plays a key role in this process.

[32]

First, the father who is present in the life of his infant begins influencing the child's initial awareness of self-identity. The father is a second significant other in the child's life, helping the newborn to begin to put healthy distance between itself and its mother. The father's presence in the newborn's life builds an awareness that there are other people in the world and helps form in the new baby's mind the sense that he or she might be one of these separate individuals.

The second significant stage of father involvement comes when the child is at the approximate age of eighteen to twenty-four months. At this time the child is forming its gender identity. We are all sensitive by now to the fact that even though gender is biologically given, gender identities can be confused in young children if parenting does not go well. Fathers play an absolutely critical role in the healthy formation of gender identity in children.

Charles Socarides says that of the four hundred homosexual men he has counseled, two-thirds suffer from acute gender confusion traceable to their experience of "crushing mothers" and "abdicating fathers." He writes, "The fathers' . . . availability is a major requirement for the development of gender identity in his children, but for almost all prehomosexual children the father is unavailable as a love object for the child."[4]

The crushing mother will not let go of her child. A mother can develop an unhealthy dependence on her child. She comes to need the relationship more than the child does. She smothers the child or emotionally dominates the child's life and inhibits the natural growth of her son or daughter toward mature individuality.

Weak fathers are unable to help toddlers suffocating in the mother bond. The abdicating father is aloof, uninvolved or absent. Some fathers are abusive. The abusive father—or the strict disciplinarian who shows no warmth of love—drives the child away. This child will tend to cling to the mother and feel abandoned by the father. The natural process of separation from the mother bond is inhibited.

[33]

At this stage in a child's development, mothers need to refrain (in love) from smothering their children while allowing and encouraging fathers to be physically and emotionally present in the lives of their sons and daughters. Children need the loving involvement of both parents. The differences between the good mother's mothering and the strong father's fathering help children experience their distinctive gender identities. They begin to see themselves not only as individuals, but as little individual boys and girls.

During these early transitions, the emotional need for fathers is so compelling that children exhibit a kind of "father hunger." It's as though they are drowning, trying desperately to reach shore, and the father is a lifeguard sent to rescue them. Recent research by psychologist Michael Lamb has shown that when toddlers are not tired or under stress, fathers are usually the preferred parent of these young children.[5] Others point out that "daddy" is often the first word children speak and that it is the father's picture, not the mother's, which attracts the child at this stage. Children who are abandoned by their fathers during this critical time can suffer deep emotional trauma and severe nightmares.[6]

During the elementary years, both boys and girls continue to need a friendly and supportive father. Boys with strong and loving fathers will find it easier to let go of their mothers and identify with their fathers. For his daughter a father wants to be affirming and accepting while communicating in a natural way his obvious love for her mother, his wife, with a deep commitment to the marriage bond. This way the father can confirm his daughter's femininity and personhood without creating any emotional confusion. A loving father can help his daughter make a healthy separation from her mother while keeping mother love intact. This will open the way for a daughter to more easily identify with her mother and later receive her mother as an adult friend.[7]

The final step in this individuation process is the transition from adolescence to adulthood. It is the final stage, when both sons and daughters keenly feel the need to fight free of the strong mother bond that has dominated their psyches from the womb. This is a very hard time for mothers. A mom will generally feel unfairly treated, especially if she is unaware of the developmental dynamics going on around her. She has always loved her children deeply, and now all they want to do is yell at her. In the face of this, some moms try to love their sons and daughters even more, showering them with attention. What such a mother does not realize is that the more she smothers during this stage, the angrier her kids will get. They do not know what is going on inside them, but they intensely feel the need to be free. They will often react violently against a mother's apparent attempts to hold them rather than let them go. This letting go is very difficult for a mom, because she is deeply aware that the kids will soon be gone. It is natural to try to hang on. But she must let them go.

Mothers may also find it difficult, and even unfair, that at this stage fathers become more important than ever to their children. Even a father who has been virtually absent from his daughter's life until now will suddenly become the focus of all her attention. A father who has been tough and abusive toward his son will often become the central figure in his life during this final transition. A mother can express unconditional love to her adolescent kids and they will treat her like dirt. The father can ignore or even hurt the kids, treating them like dirt, and they may treat him like a king. It is the final dance in this dramatic last step in breaking away.

Again, the healthy posture of the father will be affirmation of his son or daughter, but complete dedication to their mother and the marriage relationship. A father needs to listen well to the kids but keep affirming Mom. Remember, this is a temporary stage. Adolescents will say many things they don't really understand or mean. Fathers need to keep affirming Mom so that once the kids pass through this stage, they will find it easy to see the wonderful qualities in their mother that have marked her love all along the way. If the father criticizes her at the same time the kids are trying to break free, he can spoil the possibility of the children reestablishing adult friendships with their mother as they move ahead in life.

A wise father will recognize that it is not because he is such a great man that the kids need him so strongly. He must keep his ego in check. This is a stage where an ignorant and insecure man will misread a daughter's attention. What a daughter needs most is a father who will receive and acknowledge her love while showing her in no uncertain terms that his romantic loyalties lie with her mother. The strong man will lift his daughter to the next stage, individual womanhood, where she has both broken through the mother bond and successfully put to rest all childishly romantic notions about her father. Now she can freely seek relationships with male peers. She can relish the good relationship she has with her father and, as a whole and healthy young woman, can nurture a loving adult friendship with her mother.

A father who commits incest with his adolescent daughter cruelly takes advantage of the power dynamics occuring at this stage in their relationship and destroys his child. At the very moment in her life when she needs more than ever to love and accept herself as a whole and healthy adult, her father's sinful, selfish act buries her in shame. This one act shatters every significant relationship in a child's life, including the possibility of easily relating with her mother in the future. The act also destroys what might have been a beautiful, ongoing relationship with her father. Incest drives shame deep into the core of a daughter's being, inhibiting her ability to love and accept herself. She will struggle to establish a healthy sexual relationship with her husband when she marries. Most women who have been sexually abused also struggle to accept and trust the love of Father God.

Why Is a Father's Love So Significant?
During the adolescent transition, a young man or woman needs to move beyond narcissism to self-acceptance. Adolescents are

consumed by self-consciousness during this time of moving from their comfortable identity as a child to their new identity as a young man or woman.

Young men and women at this stage wonder who they really are. Questions like *Am I loved? Am I worth anything?* are ever-present. These questions will haunt them on into their adult life unless their self-identity is affirmed in a genuine way by someone significant in their life. If a young boy can discover as he grows into his manhood that he is loved and valued by a significant other, then he is freed forever from a torturous life of self-absorption. Now that he knows he is loved, he can forget about himself and shift his concerns in life toward loving others.

A mother can affirm her children in this powerful way, but they will have a harder time receiving her affirmation as authentic during the adolescent transition. It is the bond with the mother from which they are trying to break free. They will tend to resent or ignore her affection rather than receive it. Most children have never experienced a time when they wondered whether their mother loved them. It is easy to take a mother's love for granted. So the power of the mother's love to affirm the individuality of her children as they grow toward adult self-acceptance is diminished.

My sense is that most kids have always felt secure in their mother's love, but have been reaching out for the love of their father. I believe this is the key to the power of the father's love. Children view their father's love as a choice rather than a given. The emotional reality they experience when the father affirms them is that they have been chosen in love. It is this sense of choosing that puts the power of authenticity in the loving words and actions of a father.

The child wonders, *What does he think of me? Can I get close to him? Will he turn me away? Does he accept me? Does he see me? Does he believe in me? Is he proud of me? Am I special to him?* The most powerful words spoken in the New Testament might be the words of God the Father at the baptism of his Son,

"This is my Son, whom I love; with him I am well pleased" (Mt 3:17). Children need to hear this often from their fathers. As fathers who recognize the unique power of our love and affection, we too should be saying with great sincerity, "You are my son. I love you. I am so proud of you." We need to be saying often, "You are my daughter. I love you. You make me proud to be your dad."

Grandfathers can say the same things to their grandchildren. This is especially critical in single-parent homes where fathers are absent. Coaches and teachers can affirm young men and women who desperately need to know the acceptance of a significant other. Older brothers can make a huge difference in a younger brother or sister's life. A wise and loving stepfather can become a mentor in this way.

The most important thing for a single mom to realize is that she will need to nurture her children toward independence if they are going to become healthy adults. This is a hard job, especially since the father is out of the home. But the perceptive mother can do this job well if she realizes the dynamics operating here and does not give in to the temptation to smother now that the father is absent.

One Good Dad

I said earlier that the key roles of the good father are to be involved with his children rather than aloof, to be assertive and strong in a healthy, loving manner and to show his children how to affectionately sustain a meaningful long-term commitment to one woman—the children's mother—in marriage. My father was not perfect, but he was effective in these basics, and for this I will always be grateful. His good fathering gave me something significant to pass on to my children. I wrote him this Father's Day letter in 1984 to say thank you to him for his good fathering. It is the best way I know to help picture in concrete ways how good fathering is passed on to successive generations.

Dear Dad,

It's a sunny day here at the cottage. I've been sitting on the beach watching my kids play and thinking about the fact that Father's Day is coming up this weekend. I decided to write and tell you what it meant for me to grow up with you as my father. There are so many significant things you've passed on to me; so much that's good.

The highlights of my childhood were all those times that you carved out of your busy schedule just to be with us. I remember sitting close to you on the sofa every Sunday afternoon, listening to *The Shadow* and *The Green Hornet* on the radio. And when the shows were done, we'd roll around on the floor wrestling, or pretend sword fight with the cardboard centers of coat hangers. One Sunday afternoon you must have made a hundred paper airplanes of every conceivable design. Then we colored them together and flew them all around the house for hours.

Terry and I knew you enjoyed these times as much as we did, and because of that I'll never forget it. I want to be with my kids in the same fun ways.

Then there were the things you would make and do for us. You built a swing set out back on 27th Street. Nobody we knew had swings like that—steel pipe welded together and cemented into the ground. I still remember going with you to Max's junkyard to get the pipe: the smells in the shed of oil and rust, the thick dust on everything. The swing set is still there behind the house, thirty years later. We drove by it on vacation and showed our kids what Grandpa had made when I was a kid.

Another memory I have is that of sitting in the sawdust on the concrete floor one summer morning watching you turn the garage into a bedroom for us. You knew how much we enjoyed playing shuffleboard, so you tiled one in for us to play in our own bedroom. On that specific warm day, I remember handing you the nails. The Milwaukee Braves were on the radio (I can

[39]

still hear the sound of Earl Gillespie's voice). . . . Suddenly you'd stop hammering. Eddie Matthews or Hank Aaron had hit another home run.

Now my boys hand me the nails and the screws. I know what they're thinking. They're proud of me, amazed that I can make things take shape the way I do. I learned it from you. They want to grow up and build things; I can see it in their faces. And they love to work with me just as I did with you.

You were always teaching us important things, too. In sports, you demonstrated not just the skills to play the games, but the right attitudes toward others and how to treat them fairly. Competition is good, you explained, but winning isn't the most important thing. What I teach my kids now, the words I say in encouragement, the way I show them how to hold the bat, all are echoes of your voice coming through me. That's how I learned to love good play. I hope that I can give your brand of patient, enthusiastic encouragement to my own kids.

How many times did you lie on the floor and let us stand in the palms of your hands, lifting us high into the air? "Don't look down," you'd say. "Look straight ahead." We trusted you. Up we would go. Then you'd flip Terry and me off your knees and over your head, again and again, until we were so dizzy we couldn't go on. I've never come up with better tricks to do. My kids are all crazy about being flipped. They think *I'm* great, but I got it all from you. I feel like a funnel through which your good fathering flows.

I have other memories, too. I can almost feel those frigid mornings on the Mississippi, skipping along the top of the icy water in our aluminum boat, heading for our favorite small-mouth bass lake. Remember the day we hit that big bass with our propeller?

When I'd get a backlash after a bad cast, you'd let me fish with your rod and reel while you worked on mine. And sometimes I'd foul your reel before you even got mine untangled.

You'd just remind me then of some things I might be forgetting to do. I remember the fine look on your face when we'd drift along the calm surface of the lake as the sun peaked up over the horizon. I love the outdoors because you loved it and showed us your feeling about the beauty of it all. You taught us to value God's creation.

This morning Jason caught a pretty good walleye from the shore here before breakfast. I thought he was going to lose it a dozen times, but he finally dragged it in. You can imagine the look on his face as he held it up for us all to see.

Gabriel has fished for hours without a bite; but he doesn't seem a bit discouraged. I used to stand at the end of the dock at Balsam Lake just as I see him doing today—patient, steadfast, cast after cast, fishing on into the night. The mosquitoes make no difference at all. There is a lot of you in me, and a lot of me in him.

So many images are coming back. When I was little, I would sneak into your room at night, slip under the covers, snuggle up close to your warm body and sleep with my head on your powerful arm. With a father this strong and warm and close, who could ever hurt me? How could I ever be afraid? Now I know why my kids want to hold my hand, and why they like to sneak into my bed at night and sleep with their heads on my arm.

Dad, you gave us your life—everything you had. I pray that I will be able to give myself to my own children in the same way. If I can, Jana, Joshua, Jason and Gabriel will grow up to teach *their* boys and girls what it means to love, passing me on through their lives the way I have passed you on through mine.

I wish you the very best Father's Day!

With all my respect and grateful love.

Your son,

Tom

My dad did a lot of things right. He was an involved father. He had time for us. He was a good teacher and model. He included us in his life. He was verbally affirming and a strong, warm man who held hands, put his arm around us and hugged easily. And he modeled to all six of us, his six children, what it meant to be committed to a woman in marriage.

My dad became a Christian late in life. He died suddenly of a heart attack in the spring of 1992. He and my mom had been married forty-nine years. At his memorial service I spoke to the family of the visual image that came to my mind. I had this picture of Jesus lying back with his hands extended behind his head, palms up. I could see my dad stepping into the hands of Jesus, just as we had stepped into Dad's hands so many times and trusted him to lift us up. I could hear Jesus saying, "Don't look down, Bob. Look straight ahead." And that is the way Dad left us. That is the way he was lifted up.

Unique Roles of the Father

John W. Miller, in *Biblical Faith and Fathering,* traces the roots of the father-involved family to our Jewish heritage. He notes that a father's involvement in family life did not naturally come about in human culture, but was born and became a reality in families only as Israel came to experience God as a caring, redemptive Father (Is 63:16). The role of fathers in their families was strengthened and solidified as Israel carefully reenacted powerful and memorable family rituals to celebrate how God acted in their past. These rituals were presided over by fathers who took seriously their involvement in the lives of their children and families.[8]

It seems that this deep involvement of fathers in the spiritual oversight of the home is missing today in many Christian families and is not emphasized in many of today's churches. There is a rich and beautiful heritage in the father's teaching rituals in Israel. It is important to remember the ongoing and active responsibility fathers took in providing spiritual leadership within the family by regularly enacting these meaningful celebrations. As Christian fathers we need to involve ourselves more completely in teaching the foundational truths about our faith in Christ and about how God our Father is lovingly involved in our families' lives.

Years ago Judie and I were part of a small, conservative fellowship where it was common practice for fathers who wanted to be spiritually involved to baptize their children when they came to faith. I'll never forget the visual impact of being at those baptisms where a young woman or young man professed faith in Christ and then was lowered into the water and raised up again by his or her own father. The picture created by this symbolic burial and resurrection presided over by a loving father was enormously powerful and memorable to all those observing and to the sons or daughters experiencing the baptism conducted in this way.

Are there faith rituals in your family over which you as a father preside? Even reading the Gospel birth narratives at Christmas, or the resurrection story before Easter dinner, can be part of a father's family involvement. Fathers need to take leadership in spiritual matters and model their caring and protection of the family as our Father God cares for and protects us as his children. If you are not involved in this way, begin today thinking about creating regular opportunities for spiritual, fatherly involvement. As a father, be willing to preside over family faith celebrations that focus on key Christian truths or high times in the Christian calendar.

The New Testament emphasizes the uniqueness of the father's role. The apostle Paul says, "Fathers, do not exasperate your children; instead, bring them up in the training and instruction of the Lord" (Eph 6:4). If you are going to be a Christian father, a faithful leader in your home, then you will have to be a growing Christian yourself. If you want your children to love the Lord, then you must love the Lord with all your heart. If you want your children to turn to God in prayer, then you must be a man of prayer.

[43]

Don't always defer to your wife in spiritual things, even if these aspects do appear to come more easily to her than they do to you. As a father you need to lead mealtime prayers often. If you're not sure how to pray, then swallow your pride and get with someone you know who can teach you how to pray, and learn about it. Don't let your pride stand in the way of doing what's right. If you want your children to know God's Word, the Bible, then you will need to be a student of the Word. If that means you have to get into Bible Study 101, then that's where you need to be. You cannot pretend to be the spiritual leader of your family. You need to lead, to model caring fatherly involvement by bringing your children up in the training and instruction of the Lord.

Fathers are called to live out the biblical role of priest through their influence as spiritual leaders in their families (Ex 19:5-6; Is 61:6; 1 Pet 2:9). Listen to the words of Psalm 78:2-4:

I will open my mouth in parables,
    I will utter hidden things, things from of old—
what we have heard and known,
    what our fathers have told us.
We will not hide them from their children;
    we will tell the next generation
the praiseworthy deeds of the LORD,
    his power, and the wonders he has done.

The biblical father is the link between his child's present development and the Christian family faith history. The father who takes this role seriously and fulfills it lovingly will powerfully impact the lives of his children, who will very likely influence their own children in this same memorable way.

Both parents have to be significantly involved in the spiritual growth of their children. I emphasize the father's role here because we have lost our focus as fathers. We have given ourselves to the god of business rather than the God of the universe. Children who hear only their mothers pray, see only their mothers reading the Bible, go to church only with their mothers are learning that Christian belief is a mother's thing. If a father is weak in his spiritual leadership, sons will be especially quick to give up their belief when they come of age. Fathers who take little interest in spiritual matters teach their sons that spirituality is the exclusive domain of women—that real men (like their fathers) don't take part in such feminine interests.

Fathers and mothers should both be there to answer questions that children have about spiritual matters. Fathers and mothers will both want to tuck their children in at night and pray with them about their needs and concerns. Fathers and mothers will both want to pray blessings at mealtimes and take part in family devotional times that are natural to their family style. Fathers will want to find significant faith celebrations and traditions that they preside over, through which they minister to the spiritual needs of their families.

Rites of Passage

Something else is missing in the modern world that was almost always present in preindustrial societies. We now have no effective initiation of our young men into manhood. A community event that publicly acknowledges the entrance of young men into adulthood is desperately needed. For young men of the Jewish faith, this event is the bar mitzvah.

My three boys were baptized into Christ in a California swimming pool among a large gathering of fellow Christians. I was impressed at how significantly affected the boys were. I talked with them ahead of time about their new level of commitment, about baptism as a crossing over for them to a mature and responsible, personal faith. We talked about being one with the body of believers. How much of this they will remember I do not know. But the experience of being prayed for, being baptized and being warmly greeted in the community of believers present was powerful for them. Adult baptism was for them an experience that marked stepping into the future and leaving their childhood faith behind.

[45]

It was an event they can point to and say, "On that day I became a man in Christ."

My suggestion is that Christian men need to put some creative thought into what might be a meaningful rite of passage (not necessarily baptism) for young men, to mark their progress and initiate them into the Christian community of adult men. I am not saying that a rite of passage will automatically make men of our boys. If young men have not been affirmed by their fathers all along and encouraged by loving male mentors, no initiation rite can be a guaranteed fix. But if young men have known the strong and kind love of older men, especially their fathers, a ceremonial rite of passage can lock in for them the deep sense of being accepted by the community of men and affirmed as having reached a significant level of mature manhood.

The fathers of the young men gathered for such an occasion can speak with pride about their sons and identify each young man's unique qualities and gifts. Prayers can focus on the crossing over to adult faithfulness. These young adults can be affirmed as *men* of God. The men gathered for such a ceremony would be those who have already been committed as mentors to the development of these kids. Personalized, meaningful mementos could be given to each young man. The young men might also be given the opportunity to say what is on their minds.

Our churches need to make this a significant focus of their ministries. We need to create meaningful initiation rites for our young men to mark their growing maturity, affirm their masculinity and confirm their acceptance into the community of men.

I have emphasized fathers and sons here only because I think this is where the greatest deficit is today. It is young men who need the greatest encouragement to become healthy and whole, secure in their masculinity. Only in this way will they become mature fathers in their own families. The natural result of building healthier men and fathers will be a new generation of sons and daughters who know who they are and accept themselves because they have been affirmed in love by their fathers.

Tempted to Hate Your Father

We cannot pass on to our sons and daughters what we have not experienced ourselves. If we are insecure, we will tend to pass on that insecurity. It is extremely difficult to pass on to our children a secure sense of identity that we ourselves do not possess. So what can we do if we carry wounds from our fathers, wounds that have not healed? How can we be healed?

One thing is sure. If you hate your father, you will struggle to love yourself. Your father is a significant part of who you are. Your father's life has been passed on to you. Your father lives in you both through his genetic influence and in all of the life patterns you have internalized from his fathering style. If you hate your father who lives outside of you, you will also hate your father who lives within you. This is why you get so upset when you say something and sound just like your dad, or when you react to something exactly the way he would have reacted.

If you are ever to be free to love and accept yourself, you will have to break the bonds that hating your father imposes. This healing will have to take place in order for you to truly love yourself, and then to be able to genuinely love and affirm your sons and daughters. I believe this healing is possible. I have watched it take place in my wife, Judie, over the years.

At a family conference Judie shared this moving testimony about the painful early memories she had of her father and how God helped her grow toward acceptance and finally forgiveness of her father.

The earliest years were full of bad memories of my father. I have vivid memories of my father beating my mother, others, my brother. My early years were sad and unhappy times.

I loved my father, yet I hated him for what he was doing. My mother divorced my dad when I was nine. We were supposed to see him every Sunday afternoon. The first Sunday he came.

The second Sunday he came. After that I remember waiting for him, but he didn't come. For a long, long time I waited. And I hated him even more, because he didn't come.

I remember the day my mother died. My brother and sister had me call Dad. I was the youngest (eleven years old), and they thought I could talk to him. I called and said, "Daddy, we need some money."

He said, "Well, I sent the check."

I said, "I know, Daddy, but we can't cash it. Momma died this morning."

And I hated him. I went to school and got good grades, and I thought, *I will show him. I will show him what I am.* I was very independent. I was voted senior of the year in my class. There was a big banquet for me and others being honored. I called my dad and asked him if he would come. He didn't.

My father was never at anything we were a part of through the years. My sister told everyone that her father was dead. They never knew that she even had a father. All that time I knew I hated him, but I loved him too. There was this tearing inside of me.

When Tom and I got married, I needed constant affirmation from him. I didn't trust men. I had not seen a good marriage. When I became a Christian, after several years of marriage, I discovered what it was to be forgiven by God. I knew and deeply felt his forgiveness. I started reading the Bible. I got the message that I was to forgive others as God had forgiven me. I realized that this included my dad. I needed to forgive my father.

God did not ask me to forgive my dad all at once. Months would go by when I didn't think much about my dad. And then suddenly I would read a story, or see a movie, or have a conversation that would trigger something inside me. Or I would be reading Scripture and something would come into my mind that reminded me of the hurt, the pain of something terrible my dad had done.

I would often start to cry. I would think about it, cry about it, get it all out. Tom and I would talk it through. But then I would pray and say, "Jesus, you gave your life for me so that I could be forgiven. Help me to choose to forgive my dad for what he did. I choose through your power to forgive my dad."

It's strange, but at those times I would often gain insight into my dad's personality that I had never seen before. Little by little, I was able to understand. Then I could let it go and put it behind me.

Some time later, often months later, something else would come up and I'd have to go through the whole process again. Every time it was painful. But each time, a little at a time, I was able to say, "I forgive this man."

My dad, of course, never knew any of this was going on. Except after a while I would call and talk. At first he seemed a little shocked. After a while, he seemed different. There was something new in the way we talked. Some of the tension and pressure was gone.

He told me during one call that he and his wife Jane were thinking about driving out to Colorado to visit us. I was excited and scared. We had a good visit, though my dad was still stiff and emotionally distant. He enjoyed our children, which helped a lot. When they left after a week-long visit, I decided to hug my dad. Just before he got in the car I just reached out and hugged him. It was like hugging a board. He did not respond. I still said, "Daddy, I love you."

The moment I said those words, I realized that I really did love him. God had been doing an amazing work in eleven years of healing those memories. Dad said nothing. He kind of grunted, got into his car and drove away. But I knew I had done what I wanted to do and it was real for me.

The next fall I flew to Green Bay, Wisconsin, for a nephew's wedding. I was there for three days. I got there on Friday; the wedding was on Saturday. My sister had gotten tickets for me to go to a Packers game on Sunday. It was the only day I could visit Dad. I gave up the game to spend the afternoon with him. My dad knew it.

We had an excellent visit. We had time to visit my mom's grave, to pray there, to talk some about those early years, what they were like for him. It was the best time I could ever remember having with my dad.

When I was ready to go, he walked me to the car, which was very unusual. He kind of stood around for a while. But then, finally, he grabbed me, and hugged me, and said, "I love you, Honey."

This was the first time in my life, over forty years, that I heard those words from my dad. God had worked a miracle in my relationship with my father. God had given me enough strength to forgive my dad in bite-sized pieces until my heart received the healing that would allow me to reach out to my dad. My forgiveness of him freed him to become a different person toward me. The love I expressed toward him gave him the courage to reach out to me. It freed him to be daddy to me. I finally had the daddy I had wanted all my life. There is no greater gift from God than this kind of healing.

I remember meeting Judie at the airport—how she ran up to me with tears in her eyes, saying, "He said he loved me. He said he loved me." It was such a great testimony to what God can do if we are willing to take even little steps of faith toward forgiving our fathers when they have hurt us or left us with deep scars.

Sometimes Judie and her father will be talking now on the phone and I'll get on to say hello. If I try to say goodby without giving the phone back to Judie, Chet stops me. He will not hang up without saying goodby to Judie and telling her again that he loves her. I have observed another miracle from God. It is the miracle of how forgiveness can heal two people and set them free.

I know that many of you have been trampled, mocked, shamed

or abused by your fathers. You hate the man who hurt you. You may even struggle to accept God as your heavenly Father because your earthly father has hurt you so. Or you may doubt God's love because of what he allowed to happen in your life.

I could never point a finger at you and tell you that your inability to rise above your anger is a sin. Not after what you've been through—neglect, verbal and physical abuse, even molestation or incest. But I can with great courage hold out to you the hope of a miraculous healing taking place within you. You may yet be in for a divine surprise, a resurrection of love and forgiveness. I have watched this transformation take place with Judie and her dad. I know this is possible for you.

If your heart has been trampled, you can get locked in at that stage of your pain and not be able to get past it. You guard yourself. You will not open yourself to be hurt like that again. The problem is, these defenses are not selective. Once they go up, everything is kept out, the good and the bad. You won't be hurt like that again. But you won't be touched by love, forgiveness and healing either.

Our God is a God of miracles. I believe that God can heal poisoned memories if you're open to the possibility. Prayer is an obvious first step. Prayer can begin to soften your heart. The seeds of love and forgiveness cannot take root in the trampled soil of a hardened heart. Prayer can begin to soften your heart so the seeds of love can germinate there. God can create softness there, in that field of pain, so love can grow again. God can help you extend your hand in love to an enemy—even if the enemy is a member of your own family.

In prayer think of what your father might have been if he had received the love and healing of Christ that you now know as God's gift. Perhaps you can even receive that healing for your father as he lives in you. Even now his life can be redeemed in you by God's grace and power. You can begin to love the man who is in your genetic structure, the man you inherited, your father.

[51]

God can make your father a new man in you.

Whether your father is dead or alive, God can help you to forgive him. As you recognize how much he needed the love of Christ, and how powerless he was in this deep need to express the love you so desperately needed, you may even find grace to accept your father. As you pray about this you may even realize that apart from the love of Jesus, you would be just like your father.

If your father is alive today, try to see him through God's eyes, as God intended him to be. Whenever you get a glimpse of who he might have been and even still could be, thank God for it. Tell your father what you see. Pray, "Father God, love my earthly father through me." When you can pray this prayer, new life will grow in you. You will find that love begins to grow, and you will be free for the first time to really love yourself.[9]

If you struggle because you have not known the father of your dreams, turn to God your heavenly Father who wants to love you without reserve and receive you as his own. God is your Father, *Abba,* your daddy (Rom 8:15). Receive him as Daddy today. Then go out with confidence to claim your earthly and heavenly inheritance in him. First John 3:1 says, "How great is the love the Father has lavished on us, that we should be called children of God! And that is what we are!" Praise God, our heavenly Father, for his great love for us.

Questions for Discussion

1. Briefly describe for others what comes to mind when you think about your father.

2. Do you agree with the author that we are experiencing a fathering crisis in this generation? What realities have caused and are perpetuating the problem of absentee fathers?

3. How does a father's presence in the home help children to develop their gender identity?

4. Why is the adolescent transition a particularly painful time for some mothers? What insights from the chapter might encour-

[52]

age moms who feel hurt or unfairly treated by their kids during this time?

5. According to the chapter, how can fathers be most helpful to their children and their children's mother during the adolescent transition?

6. What were some of the good qualities the author recognized in his dad as he wrote the Father's Day letter? What were some good qualities you remember about your father?

7. If you are a father, do you preside over any Christian celebrations or family events? If so, describe the events and what role you take in these family learning experiences or traditions.

8. Is there anyone in your family whom you find it hard to love, to forgive? If you feel comfortable doing so, tell who this person is and explain why it has been hard to love and forgive in this case. Then pray together for each other, that there could be healing in these troubled relationships, that forgiveness and love could grow again.

3
Tempted to Wonder—
Is Being a Mom
Worth the Trouble?

•

God is at work in a unique and powerful way through a mother's love. Thomas Carlisle once said, "I tried to get away from the Christian faith, but my mother's life was too much for me." The apostle Paul acknowledges the powerful influence a grandmother and mother had on his coworker Timothy when he writes, "I have been reminded of your sincere faith, which first lived in your grandmother Lois and in your mother Eunice and, I am persuaded, now lives in you also" (2 Tim 1:5). The believing mother has the capacity to make a profound impact on her children regarding their eternal life in Christ.

One night while our family was watching a TV program, our son Gabe, who was about nine at the time, wandered off to the other end of the room. There he sat down at the desk and started typing on the family computer. After the kids went to bed that night Judie and I noticed the computer was still on. As I went over to shut it off, I found what Gabe had written and left on the screen:

Jesus is the only God that lives and shall not die. He shall live forever and ever. He is our Savior. He who believes in him will have eternal life. I love him very much, and I will never forget him for all my living life, and he shall never forget us.

Where does a fourth-grade boy get such a deep sense of security in Christ? I believe that to a great extent it's the result of good mothering. A secure faith in a loving God comes naturally to those who experience the unconditional, consistent and dependable love of a mother. That kind of genuine love permeates and blesses a home.

The Value of Motherhood Called into Question

If you take a tour of any library and glance through books on family life written before the mid-sixties, a consistent message emerges. Mothers were held in the highest esteem. Volume upon volume describes the mother as having the most significant influence in her child's life. She is seen as a loving nurturer and a significant spiritual leader who powerfully shapes her child's values.

But times have changed. Popular writing in the last several decades has called into question the essential value of motherhood and whether the sacrificial commitment required to be a mother in today's world is really worth it. Being a mom—especially a mom and homemaker—is just not "in" today. It's not fashionable. Women who are "with it" today are primarily concerned with full-time careers outside the home, working their way up corporate ladders and dressing for success. At social gatherings they talk with other "successful" women about old friends and classmates who got stuck in a marriage with kids before finding out how wonderful life in the fast lane could really be.

In a newspaper interview, one mom, Kay King, says that the price she paid for choosing to be a full-time mother was snubs from professional women. When her husband worked as a White House Fellow in Washington, the Kings needed to involve themselves in the D.C. social circuit. Invariably she would be asked the question "And what do you do?" She said the answer "I'm at home with my children" always stopped conversation cold.

[55]

"There were times when I wanted to shake them and say, 'I'm not stupid. Don't worry about sitting next to me at the dinner table. I'm not going to reach over and cut your meat into a thousand pieces.' "[1]

There is much about motherhood that is not glamorous in the least. A mom may be up at 6:00 a.m. to begin her nonstop day. She will set out breakfast for the family and then pack lunches, scrub faces, coach last-minute unfinished homework, chauffeur children, change diapers, mix baby formula, scrub floors, wash windows, do laundry, scour the bathrooms and toilets, feed the hamster, let the cat out, let the cat in, let the plumber into the neighbor's house, cheer the soccer team, bandage scrapes, wipe noses, be a den mother, fix dinner, do dishes, attend school meetings, send a Mother's Day card to her mother-in-law, referee sibling fights, bathe children, read them stories and tuck them in, finish some accounting work for her home business, sew on a couple of buttons, put the finishing touches on a devotional for her small group Bible study in the morning, and fall into bed at midnight. If a mom has to work outside the home, she will generally be trying to keep up with all this by cramming it into her second shift, the shift that begins the instant she walks in the door from work. It was probably a day like this that prompted one young mother to say to me, "It's amazing that you have so much to do in a day and seem to have so little to show for it."

Caught up in the often frantic pace of motherhood, it is easy to lose perspective, to forget what it's really all about and what makes it all worthwhile. It's true that there are no degrees granted for good mothering, no promotions given, no salary. But it's a mistake to think of motherhood in these terms, as if a mother's value could be measured in dollars and cents.

There is a deeply embedded misconception in our society about how people should be valued. Even the sensitive journalist who interviewed Kay King felt it was necessary to list her academic credentials first to authenticate her value as a person—her Ph.D.

in linguistics from UCLA, Phi Beta Kappa, Phi Kappa Phi, graduation magna cum laude, and University of Utah Woman of the Year. Otherwise people might not have read on to find out what she had to say about the significance of being a mother.

It's a strange value system that suggests gaining a degree at a university or even graduating with honors is more important than raising a child or creating a stable home environment full of resilient love, learning and nurture. No, there is no salary for being a mother, and there are no promotions. Nor should there be. The truth is that what a mother is and does cannot be measured in economic terms. What a mother does is nothing less than fulfill the highest calling known to humankind. It would be perverse to think that the value of this sacrificial work, so vital to the ongoing life and health of the human community, could be measured monetarily.

This is why I paid so little attention to the article circulating awhile back that tried to measure motherhood by putting a dollar-per-hour amount on all a mother's household tasks. It just doesn't work. A mother's contribution can't be summed up by punching out the holes on a time card. It would be like trying to put a monetary value on the work of Mother Teresa. The kind of work a mother chooses in the home, a deep and selfless commitment to serving others with her life, won't submit to cost effectiveness.

Do we need a list of worldly credentials ahead of *mother* and *homemaker* to validate the worth of women in the home today? No! Motherhood needs no outside props to make it valid.

The Significance of the Mother's Role

In his book *Sexual Suicide* George Gilder gives us a contemporary and accurate statement of the importance of mothers and wives. He writes,

> The central position of the woman in the home parallels her central position in all civilized society. Both derive from her necessary role in procreation and from the most primary and

[57]

inviolable of human ties, the one between mother and child. In those extraordinary circumstances when this tie is broken—as with some disintegrating tribes—broken as well is the human identity of the group. Most of the characteristics we define as humane and individual originate in the mother's love for her children.

Deriving from this love are the other civilizing concerns of maternity: the desire for male protection and support, the hope for stable community life, and the aspiration for a better future. The success or failure of civilized society depends on how well the women can transmit these values to the men, to whom they come less naturally. . . . The males have no ties to women and children—or to long-term community—so deep or tenacious as the mother's to her child. That is primary in society, all else is contingent and derivative. . . .

The woman's place in the scheme is deeply individual. She is valued for her uniqueness. Only a specific woman can bear a specific child, and her tie to it is personal and infrangible. When she raises the child she imparts in privacy her own individual values. She can create children who transcend consensus and prefigure the future; children of private singularity rather than "child development policy." . . .

One of the roles of the woman as arbiter, therefore, is to cultivate herself; to fulfill her moral, aesthetic and expressive being as an individual. There is no standard beyond her. She is the vessel of the ultimate values of the society. The society is what she is and what she demands in men. She does her work because it is of primary rather than instrumental value. The woman in the home with her child is the last bastion against the technocratic marketplace.[2]

There is a chauvinistic flavor to Gilder's comments, but the central affirmations here are true. Mothers alone can perform the crucial act in the perpetuation of the species, the incarnation of birthing a child. Birthing and nurturing a child is the only role of unquestionable worth and importance to the human community. There will always be men and women in great numbers who are able to perform the job functions required to keep the fax paper flowing in our mega-corporations. But human society itself will crumble without the essential leadership of loving, effective mothers and wives. Everything of worth and for which we deeply care derives from motherhood. When boiled down to the essentials, there is one thing we absolutely cannot do without; we simply cannot do without mothers.

Gilder mentions the significance of the mother bond. There is no stronger natural love than the love of a mother for her children. Harold Voth of the Menninger Clinic says the studies on the significance of the mother bond in the early life of the infant are abundantly clear.[3] The most common, seemingly mundane experiences between mother and child are really the most significant of all human experiences. To be rocked and held, cuddled and kissed, kept warm and dry, and regularly orally gratified are the experiences that prevent a young child and later adult from being overwhelmed with insecurity and anxiety. If these early times do not go well, some level of diminished health and functioning in the future life of the child is virtually guaranteed.

The mother and child go on from these early experiences to a series of separations as the child is nurtured toward independence. Throughout this time a child tests the boundaries of freedom while at the same time desiring (and needing) the constant security of the mother's presence. The more deeply a child can internalize this sense of maternal security, the greater the level of healthy self-assurance that child will carry into adult life. A core of trust and courage is developed, an inner sense of never being alone, even when in solitude. The internalized presence of a good and loving mother lives on within her child's personality, bringing a continuing sense of peace and reassurance about life. If these significant processes are interfered with, the seeds of emotional illness are sown quite early. We need only think of the confirmed absence of mothers in the early lives of Charles Manson and Lee Harvey Oswald to get a picture of what the result can be if this indispensable bonding and nurturing process does not occur.

This is the most disturbing aspect of the current breakdown of the family and the negative press generated toward the role of mothers in our day. Millions of babies, toddlers and young children, who are deprived of the tender care and nurture they need, will carry immaturity, a weak self-concept and a wide variety of dangerous personality disorders into their future marriages, families and the society at large.

I can't help but think here of what a powerful impact my mother made on my psyche when she carried me—her deathly sick, asthmatic little boy—slowly back and forth through our house in the middle of the night. She would hold me upright in her arms so I could breathe and sleep. Sometimes when I was very sick, this would go on for several nights in a row. My mom and dad would take shifts through the night. I have always known, deep down, that someone cared whether I lived or died.

Gilder goes on to make the important point that a wife and mother is also instrumental in encouraging her husband to willingly and joyfully participate in family life. A woman's love for her husband, and her appreciation of his commitment to fatherhood and providing for the family, helps a father realize his significance and adopt a long-term vision for the family. This long-term commitment does not come as naturally to the man as it does to the woman. A mother instinctively knows that a stable home environment is essential for children to grow up as healthy, mature adults.

The Christian woman in the home can celebrate her absolute and essential role in human society. Her personal values and character are invested in and impressed on her children, and through her children's lives will shape the very future of civilization.

Moms Who Have to Work Outside the Home
The best experience for young children is to have their mother at

home. It is critical for children to securely bond as much as possible with a primary caregiver, preferably the mother, especially during the early years. This should be the highest priority for families who have a choice. At the very least a mother needs to be with her baby for the first six months of the child's life. Even secular authorities agree that infants do not do well in day-care situations.[4]

Unfortunately, only a shrinking minority of today's moms still have complete freedom to stay at home and devote themselves solely to the concerns of motherhood. The majority of households have been hit hard by rising costs, a weakening job market and a dramatic drop in real earnings over the past two decades. During this period the cost of housing has skyrocketed 56 percent, college tuition has jumped almost 90 percent, and social security taxes have gone up 24 percent. Gallup polls show that only 13 percent of working mothers want to work full time, while 52 percent feel they have to.[5]

It is just not enough for us as evangelical conservatives to keep loading guilt on moms who have had to enter the job market to keep their families from falling desperately behind. A mom should not be made to feel guilty for this kind of dedication. We no longer live in the 1950s. What we need now is less condemnation and more creative thinking. We need to stand with each other and work together to find new ways to manage our complex families in these difficult times, with the goal of seeing to it that our children do not get shortchanged.

Judie and I struggled with this issue when we had a young family. We adopted twin boys when our daughter, Jana, was four. Jana had been in preschool, and Judie was working part time during the day. I was working full time as a teacher. Judie asked her boss if she could switch her hours and come in at night. He agreed. So Judie had the kids all day, and I got them from 4:30 to 9:00 p.m. four nights a week. This was not the best arrangement for our marriage. Judie and I often felt like strangers from our lack of time together, but it was an excellent arrangement for the kids. It allowed Judie to be the primary caregiver and kept me meaningfully involved in our young children's lives.

Both moms and dads can make excellent home parents. Many parents today are finding that they can split work inside and outside the home. This has many advantages. It models to children that both parents care about what is happening in the home and that both parents have an equal commitment to the children. Fathers and mothers who both work outside the home, while caring for their children and each other at home, are training their children to manage a more flexible family structure without giving up on the family values that make healthy families work.

If Mom has to work outside the home, then Dad has to change his attitude toward work in the home. Too many men come home from work to relax while their wives come home from work to face their second shift at home. I still catch myself saying things like "Let me help you with the dishes," as if the dishes are Judie's responsibility. No, it's all *our* responsibility—helping with the homework, running kids around, getting meals on, doing household chores—we make it all work together. And we do it because we love each other and making the family work is our highest priority.

Some moms need to get better at letting their husbands share the load at home. Some wives and mothers find it difficult to let go of the idea that work in the home is solely their responsibility and they somehow fail if they are unable to carry the entire load alone. They shouldn't have to do it alone. Household chores are for all members of the household. It may make things run more smoothly, too, if moms can accept a slightly lower level in the quality of housework accomplished by husbands and children who are learning how to take more responsibility for household chores.

I have seen families damaged by the more extreme traditional view of Mom as homemaker and Dad as breadwinner. In today's economic climate, too much can be expected of Dad. The father

[62]

who believes that the family income rests solely on his shoulders may wind up spending sixty to seventy hours a week on the job. Or he may take on a couple of part-time jobs to make ends meet. He may be doing what's expected of him as breadwinner, but he will fail as a father. Too many of us have grown up in homes where our fathers were not available to us because they were so completely tied up in their work.

On the other hand, it is also important for wives and mothers to continue to develop their unique gifts and capabilities. They need to resist the temptation to put personal growth on the back burner while they are so deeply involved as mothers. Moms need to use their gifts in a variety of ways. In this way moms can grow and feel good about themselves as well as bring new dimensions to family life. As Gilder suggests, it is important for a woman who wants to make a lasting impression on the next generation that she "cultivate herself" and "fulfill her moral, aesthetic and expressive being as an individual." If she does not, we all lose.

The problem here is thinking that a single structure will work for all families. Life is too complex to allow us to think that artificially clinging to a 1950s-style family arrangement will solve all the problems and struggles of families today. What is really needed is to revive our deep concern for family values. Holding solid, biblical values creates the foundation from which a healthy family life can emerge in any number of different possible arrangements.

Recent surveys of contemporary American families yield surprising results. Most Americans believe that traditional family values should be the basis for family life. William J. Doherty writes, "Surveys indicate that most Americans still believe in the traditional family values of responsibility and commitment, and most believe that the stable, two-parent family is the best environment for raising children."[6] There simply has to be more tolerance for families today who are struggling to find an arrangement that works for them. Flexibility in family management is needed, creative solutions to make the family project work in a social environment that is becoming increasingly hostile to family life. There are numerous legitimate family structures that can produce family integrity if there is a renewed dedication to maintaining basic family values, especially the values of mutual commitment and loving responsibility toward others.

Both men and women today have to rededicate themselves in a primary rather than secondary way to their highest priority next to their personal relationship with Christ—responsible devotion to raising their children. In this way parents will continue to raise children with character—mature children who have a solid foundation of biblical values and who walk in the security of knowing both their parents and their Savior, Jesus Christ. These young men and women will be fully equipped to face the changing demands of future life.

The Uniqueness of a Mother's Love

I have recognized a quality in Judie's love for the kids that differs in style from what comes naturally to me as their father. I have noticed that this particular quality is common among most women and mothers. It is a kind of loving that most closely approximates the agape love of God toward us.

A saying we hear often is "He's got a face only a mother could love." There is truth here that's worth exploring. We all know the natural, human kind of love that finds it easy to love lovely people. But a mother's love is often quite different.

I have always found it intriguing to watch young children with their favorite rag dolls or dirty, shredded blankets. One of our boys was so attached to his blanket that we had to sneak it away to wash it. After one of these bootleg washings, we couldn't find Jason in the house. Then we saw him out under the backyard clothesline. He was standing on tiptoe, desperately clutching the bottom of his tattered blanket, holding on for dear life.

Kids fall in love with these smelly, dirty things. The older the dolls and rags get, the worse they look, but the kids love them just the same. Other toys look better and are worth more. But the kids love their ragged blankets and dirty rag dolls. A mother's love is like this. It is more like God's love in this regard than any other human love, for a mother's love for her children does not depend on what her son or daughter looks like. It does not depend on how well he or she performs. Just as that little child loves value into a favorite rag—value that would not exist in the thing itself—our mothers love value into us, by loving us as we really are.

Who knows you better than your mother? Who knows you so well, the good and the bad, and still loves you? If you freely love others and have a resilient sense of your own value, it is probably due in large part to the gift of love your mother gave you, her ragged child. God has given us a remarkable earthly model of his own love—love with no strings attached. Many of us know God's love best simply by experiencing it firsthand through our mother's love for us.

I remember an incident that happened years ago that etched into my mind forever a picture of the uniquely Christlike love so characteristic of mothers. Joshua and Jason were incredibly excited that morning because their kindergarten class was taking a field trip to the pumpkin farm. It was a cold, wet day, so Judie dressed them in their new winter coats and sent them off to school. But when it was time for them to be home, they were nowhere to be seen. Judie kept going to the front window, watching for them to come up the street.

After a few minutes Judie got nervous and drove over to the school to find them. Heatherwood Elementary sat on a hill with a long, terraced dirt field and steep embankments leading down to the sidewalk. The field had not yet been sodded. It was nothing but red clay. In the rainy, mucky weather that clay had turned to thick, runny red mud. When Judie got to the school, there were these two little boys, dragging two of the biggest pumpkins you've ever seen, slipping and slopping through that field of mud. They'd fallen down repeatedly; that was clear. They looked like two living mud pies. Both were crying and upset. They'd struggle to get to their feet, then would topple over again, trying to push or drag or roll their prize pumpkins, desperate to get them to the street and home.

Judie's heart broke when she saw them. She climbed up the hill to where they were. She could barely see their teary eyes peeking out through faces caked with red mud. Their new coats were so covered with mud that she could not even tell which of the twins was which. She got down on her knees, took them both in her arms with a sloppy hug and simply said, "Come on. We'll get these pumpkins home."

Mothers love like this because they would not make it through the tough job of being a mom if God didn't pour out on them this kind of special love a hundred times a day. Families can be so frustrating. A mom can do everything she knows how to do, but the kids seem to show so little progress at times. She will work nonstop from dawn to midnight and at the end of the day be too weary to think of one significant thing she accomplished. Carrying the heavy load of family is a bit like trying to drag a giant pumpkin through the muck. When things get really tough, moms who are in the trenches can count on one thing. God will never say, "You should've picked a smaller pumpkin!"

God blesses our choice to have and raise children. He comes and meets us right where we are, wraps his arms around us—even though we're covered with the mud and muck of the world from head to toe—and says, "Come on. We'll get these families home." I believe Christian moms have this extraordinary capacity to demonstrate agape love in their families because they know what it's like to be given unconditional support and love on a daily, even hourly basis from God.

The Christian mother whose primary devotion is to her children and the quality of life in the home holds in her loving arms the very nature and figure of human life to come. There is no calling more important than this. No career project could ever be attempted that would be more important than helping a child to grow up mature and strong, delighting in the goodness of the Christian faith and carrying on the cause of Jesus Christ into the future of our desperately needy world.

Questions for Discussion

1. Share with your spouse or group what comes to mind when you think about your mother.

2. What cultural changes lie behind the diminishing view of the significance of motherhood?

3. Discuss the major points raised in this chapter in support of the important task of motherhood. Why are mothers vital to the family dynamic, and why is good mothering absolutely necessary for the health of human society at large?

4. The author believes that even though it is best for children to have a primary caregiver in the home, especially when they are young, it is still possible to achieve a healthy family organization through creative management in families where both parents have to work outside the home. Do you agree or disagree with this idea? If both parents are working outside the home in your family, how do you make sure your children and marriage do not suffer as a result?

5. Give examples that you have observed of the uniquely powerful, unconditional love of mothers at work.

4
Tempted to Miscommunicate:
Walking in Our Partner's
World of Meaning

•

The Wall

Their wedding picture mocked them from the table, these two, whose minds no longer touched each other.

They lived with such a heavy barricade between them that neither battering ram of words nor artilleries of touch would break it down.

Somewhere, between the oldest child's first tooth and the youngest daughter's graduation, they lost each other.

Throughout the years, each slowly unraveled that tangled ball of string called self, and as they tugged at stubborn knots, each hid his searching from the other.

Sometimes she cried at night and begged the whispering darkness to tell her who she was.

He lay beside her, snoring like a hibernating bear, unaware of her winter.

Once, after they had made love, he wanted to tell her how afraid he was of dying but, fearing to show his naked soul, he spoke instead about the beauty of her breasts.

She took a course in modern art, trying to find herself in

colors splashed upon a canvas, and complaining to other wom-
en about men who were insensitive.

He climbed into a tomb called "The Office," wrapped his mind
in a shroud of paper figures and buried himself in customers.

Slowly the wall between them rose, cemented by the mortar
of indifference.

One day, reaching out to touch each other, they found a bar-
rier they could not penetrate, and recoiling from the coldness of
the stone, each retreated from the stranger on the other side.

For when love dies, it is not in a moment of angry battle, nor
when fiery bodies lose their heat.

It lies panting, exhausted, expiring at the bottom of a wall

it

could

not

scale.[1]

A marriage will be as good as the communication that exists between its partners. A family will be as healthy as its communication is clear, honest and caring. Communication is the nervous
system of the *one flesh* relationship called marriage, and of the
living, developing organism we call the family. The life energy in
a dynamic family system grows and is positively charged as caring,
reciprocal communication happens regularly between its members. It is in the intimate sharing of lives through the pathways of
honest communication that love is known and expressed.

There is no better way to experience biblical koinonia in the
family than in sharing one another's lives in increasingly intimate
communication. Every family member needs to be known, to be
loved and to share love. Love is realized in the family when communication flows easily between all its members. When attentive
listening, unconditional acceptance and mutual respect are high,
and when fear of disclosure, misunderstanding and manipulation
are low, love has fertile ground in which to grow. The fact that
mutual, open dialogue exists in a family is a sure sign that love

is having its way. The health of a family can be measured by the quality of its communication.

The Goal of Communication

Lack of communication in families does not necessarily mean that no one is talking. A family may be talking, but not about the things that really matter. The goal of communication is to learn how to enter into each other's worlds of meaning. Real communication happens when the world of meaning of one person truly meets the world of meaning of another through the complex process of expressing oneself through words, facial expressions, vocal intonation, body language and eye contact.

Learning to better communicate with one another enhances our experience of shared love. Better communication leads to deeper levels of disclosure, where we discover the joy of honest, mutual sharing of needs, hopes, hurts and dreams. John Powell says communication begins with the low-risk talk that includes ritual clichés and the reporting of facts. From there we take greater risks by sharing our ideas, judgments and honest emotions. And finally, our communication matures to the point that we begin to enjoy "peak" experiences of absolute openness and honesty. These peak encounters result in complete communion of our personal worlds. This kind of communication is characteristically nonjudgmental, free of fear, honest in reporting emotions and fully mutual.[2]

David Augsburger sees the process as moving through seasons of maturation that begin with what he calls the *expectation stage.* The experiential filters of our past dominate this early stage of the communication process. These expectations about life and others filter what we hear and color what we say so that it is difficult for clear and open communication to take place. During this early stage it is common to resort to manipulation. We persuade, seduce, coerce, evade and avoid to get what we want.

Later, as we grow, we discover communication as *invitation.* We begin to give up manipulation as we develop the skills for and

[70]

enjoy the benefits of listening, inviting and drawing the other person out.

Mature communication for Augsburger is *dialogue*. Dialogue is honest, reciprocal, respectful communication. True dialogue includes honest disagreements but always with complete confirmation of the partner as a person. Such a level of communication is based on deep trust where each partner can risk being completely vulnerable.[3] Augsburger and Powell both believe that the ultimate aim of communication in growing relationships is to experience the honest, intimate sharing of our worlds with one another.

Why Our Words Miss the Mark

My communication goal for marriage, then, is to learn how to enter into Judie's world of meaning, hear her story, affirm her story, minister to her real needs as we share our life of mutual love. Her goal would be the same: to learn how to enter into my world of meaning and to hear, affirm and minister to the real person that is me. But this kind of communication does not happen quickly or easily. We both believe we are only beginning now to sustain this deeper level of intimacy after thirty-three years of exploring communication together in our marriage.

There are numerous barriers to achieving good communication. The first is that most of us, especially when we first enter marriage, are naive about the complexities involved in the communication process. We think it is going to be easy. We have usually been operating in a romantic mode and dealing with communication at its least risky level. Now we are living together and having to work out the deeper dimensions of managing a love relationship over a lifetime.

We may, for example, not be aware of how much communication is nonverbal. When communication goes wrong we are often surprised because we cannot imagine how the words we said became so garbled in the mind of the other person. We hear ourselves saying, "How could she/he have gotten *that* out of what I said?"

There are three elements in spoken communication: the verbal, the vocal and the visual. The verbal element is the content or words we speak. The vocal includes how we color what we say with intonation, volume and pitch. The visual elements include body language, gestures, facial expressions and eye contact. Research has shown that communication is most accurately received and believed when these three elements are congruent, that is, when all aspects are apparently saying the same thing. When there is incongruence, we send mixed messages. We miscommunicate.

We make the mistake of thinking that what counts most in communication is the words we speak. But the verbal element carries only 7 percent of our message. The vocal contributes 38 percent. And the visual accounts for 55 percent of the overall impact of what we say. Albert Mehrabian, who conducted landmark studies at UCLA on the three *V*s of spoken communication, found that when the verbal, vocal and visual elements were inconsistent, the verbal was virtually smothered by the others. We pick up far more from intonation, body language and facial expression than from the words themselves. When communication does not work for us, it is often because we are not aware of the broader and more subtle dimensions of how our communication patterns affect others.[4]

Physiological realities further complicate the process. As we speak, our message passes through a unique filtering device in the other person called the First Brain. The First Brain is the seat of human emotion. It is the most primitive portion of the brain located in the brain stem and the limbic system. From there our presentation travels to the New Brain for analytical processing. The New Brain makes up the cerebral cortex and is the seat of conscious thought, memory, language, creativity and decision-making. When we communicate we invariably aim the spoken word at the New Brain, where cognitive thinking and deciding take place. But to get to the analytical processing area, communication has to pass through the First Brain first. Researchers believe that the First Brain acts as a switching station for all sensory input and determines what will be passed on to the New Brain for analysis and what will be filtered out or ignored.

Today the First Brain sorts reality in much the same way it did in the earliest human beings. It is sniffing out the environment, asking subconscious questions like *Am I safe? Should I stay? Should I flee? Is the other person friendly? Can he be trusted?* If our nonverbal cues suggest that we are insincere, threatening or in some way projecting an image, the First Brain system alters our message in the mind of the other person. The other person receives our message and edits it according to the emotional cues being picked up. We are seldom aware of how many bits of sensory information we are giving off that are being read by the other person's First Brain.[5]

Our partners can show us how our emotions and expressions color our communication. They can help us understand why our words sometimes fail to deliver our intended meaning, even when we are sincere. When you care deeply about something, you may unconsciously raise the pitch of your voice too high and express your words with too much intensity. You think you are simply making your point clearly and with emphasis. But the intensity may come across to others as anger, or as if you are out of control and not to be trusted. You will not be heard because there is a level of threat being picked up by others.

We can learn about these aspects of our communication patterns that get in the way of open communication. We can learn how to honestly present what we think and feel so that our verbal content is congruent with our vocal and visual presentation. Appreciating these innate difficulties in communication will help us get our intended message across.

Entering Each Other's World of Meaning

Every person brings to the communication process a family history of interaction which seems normal, natural and right. Our world has created expectations we carry into all our attempts to communicate. These expectations about life and people have developed in each of us, beginning with the earliest bonding experiences and continuing throughout our childhood, adolescence and on into adult life. Most often we do not see the cultural fabric that controls the expectations we bring to our speaking and listening. It is as if we have been hypnotized by our past and now respond to certain cues that come to us the way we would respond to hypnotic suggestions.

Our life experiences establish patterned reactions to our communication environment. We simply do what we know has helped us survive in the past. The problem is, our partner (especially early in our marriage) and our children often know little about our history. They have no idea why we might react to a certain word or tone of voice or attitude.

There is a family-operated bagel bakery near my home. The bagels are great, but I love to go in as much to listen to this family interact as to eat my bagel and have my coffee. There is no attempt in this three-generation business to smooth anything over with pleasantries. And you would not be able to guess from their communication style that there might be different levels of significance in the problems they face. They simply yell at each other about everything that happens in the shop, large or small. They all bark orders at one another and criticize each other in front of customers. They complain about everything under the sun, while verbally bashing each other over every issue and topic that comes up, whether or not the other person seems interested. Each member of the family appears to participate with equal skill in the verbal sparring.

This family has an unusual way of managing their communication, to say the least. But in observing them, I sense a certain family solidarity and belonging created by their communication style. If Grandpa did not yell at you, you would feel like an outsider. You would think he didn't love you like the rest. They also operate at a surprising level of honesty. You never wonder where any member of the family stands on any issue. In many ways I find it refreshing to be in an environment where no one minces words, and yet the family bond remains strong.

I have tried to imagine, though, what will happen when one of the kids in this family marries someone else. Think of the work that would have to be done if a young man from this emotional and up-front household married a quiet young woman from a Lutheran farm community in Minnesota. No one in her family ever talked about what they thought. This was too personal. And no one ever expressed anger of any kind. Can you imagine? This young man would yell at his new wife, thinking this is the way to create a sense of family unity. It's the way it worked in his family. But she would feel invaded, criticized, bullied by his verbal intensity. I see these kinds of cultural clashes lived out in my office every week.

I have watched and listened to an electrical engineer summarize the facts as he sees them that are contributing to the relational difficulties between himself and his wife and children. With great clarity and objectivity he presents what he believes to be the truth regarding their family situation. The man lives in a world where data is analyzed and numbers are crunched according to equations that promise predictable and reproducible results. It is a world where reason and logic reign. But he fails to understand that his "objective" perspective is only unquestionably valid in the closed system of his familiar world. He believes he is right because he operates in a mathematical and scientific culture, where his "objective" methods work consistently. But there are other valid ways of seeing the world, and numerous ways of discovering what is true in a family situation.

His wife knows her husband's style of interacting is killing their relationship and hurting the children. She is aware of many practical truths about principles of open dialogue, sensitive listening and encouragement that work to build a loving family community.

[75]

These are relational truths he does not understand and needs desperately to learn. He would be wise to listen to his wife when she tells him that his arrogant posture has made real communication between himself and other family members impossible. But no one can teach him anything. He has been hypnotized by his career culture.

On our own, we find it difficult to see how our expectations color our communication because we simply live them out without thinking about them. But when we allow another person to tell us honestly about her struggles with our communication style, we can begin to loosen our grip on the unnecessary baggage from our past that hinders our present dialogue. Perhaps your father always gave you the silent treatment when he was angry. Now when your husband is quiet, you believe he must be angry with you too. But he explains that he does not have to be talking with you to feel close. This is just his way. You accept him at his word. You learn something new about your different worlds, and another level of intimacy and connection is born in your relationship.

Or perhaps when you were growing up you always found it safer to tell your alcoholic mother what she wanted to hear rather than the truth. When you tried to be honest with her, she would explode and attack you. Now you live out this pattern with your wife, and she feels distanced by it. She wants to know how you really feel, what you really want to do, what she does to you that bothers you. She can't get close to you when you tell her only what you think she wants to hear. If you truly listen to your wife and respond honestly, you will experience new freedom and take another step into the deeper intimacy you both desire.

We innocently enter into communication with another and immediately get lost and wonder why. The personal background we carry with us determines to a great extent what we say and how we say it. We can learn from sensitively interacting with others how our communication style has been formed by our past experiences and what parts of it work or do not work in our new relationships. Our background also creates a context into which another's communication falls, a context which filters what others say to us. We need to become aware of how we filter what comes in, why we react the way we do to certain words, gestures, postures, attitudes—reactions that often puzzle our spouse or children.

Those who love us can teach us where things have gone wrong, when what we heard was not what they intended to say. As these barriers come down, there will be fewer painful misunderstandings and deeper, authentic dialogue between you and the other members of your family.

Questions for Discussion

1. This chapter began with an anonymous piece called "The Wall." What feelings and attitudes expressed hit home to you? Why?

2. On a scale of one to ten (with ten being as good as it can be), how would you as an individual rate the quality of communication between you and your spouse? Compare your answers with your spouse's, and discuss any differences privately. If you are part of a larger group, let any couples who feel comfortable doing so share the content of their discussion with the rest of the group.

3. What does trust have to do with communication? How is trust built in a marriage relationship?

4. Discuss the numerous reasons that communication is difficult rather than easy. What common barriers do you think have contributed most to miscommunication in your own marriage relationship?

5. List and discuss as many reasons as you can for why communication is crucially important in a marriage and family.

5

Tempted to Ignore
the Differences Between
Men and Women

•

In a fascinating national bestseller called *You Just Don't
Understand,* Deborah Tannen contends that the key to better
communication between couples is to understand that men and
women come from and live in different worlds. They learn the
language of their gender as they grow up and communicate in their
own male or female culture.

Tannen does not write from a biblical or theological perspective,
but her work parallels some foundational biblical concepts. From
the Genesis narrative, for example, we can begin to understand
some of the differences in perspective between men and women
and why attempts to communicate with one another often fail. The
Genesis material most germane to the discussion of gender differences describes how things changed for men and women after the
Fall. When Adam and Eve suddenly realized they were naked,
they tried to cover themselves. They became self-conscious about
their sexual identities for the first time. They no longer shared the
beautiful, shameless union of "one flesh" they had before the Fall.
Sin destroyed that pre-Fall harmony they enjoyed. After the Fall
Adam and Eve experienced separation and isolation, from each
other and from God.

God tells Eve that her future relationship with Adam will be a painful struggle. He says, "Your desire will be for your husband, and he will rule over you" (Gen 3:16). Eve's sin was rooted in her desire for greater power. She wanted a position higher than God had given. She took things into her own hands because she wanted to be like God (Gen 1:28; 3:4-6). But after Eve realized the truth, she had a deep "desire," a nostalgic longing, for what was lost in sin—the relationship of shameless love and mutuality that she and Adam shared before the Fall. But she did not get what she wanted. The Hebrew word translated "desire" in this text suggests that Eve will experience an *unreciprocated longing* for her husband.

Gilbert Bilezikian explains the meaning of this word in context: [The woman's] desire will be for her husband, so as to perpetuate the intimacy that had characterized their relationship in paradise lost. But her nostalgia for the relation of love and mutuality that existed between them before the fall, when they both desired each other, will not be reciprocated by her husband. Instead of meeting her desire, he will rule over her. . . . The woman wants a mate and she gets a master; she wants a lover and she gets a lord; she wants a husband and she gets a hierarch.[1]

If Eve's sin was a desire for greater dominion, Adam's sin was a failure to exercise his dominion. If Eve will long now for the experience of mutual love and harmony lost through her sin, Adam will experience nostalgia over lost dominion, desiring to regain lost authority. But Adam's weakness now is that the dominion for which he yearns will, when he attempts to exercise it, be twisted by his fallen nature into *dominance*. This is not God's plan. It is the result of the Fall. Instead of living out a loving style of accountable authority in his relationship with Eve, his tendency will be to dominate her. He longs to regain proper authority—a gift he had before the Fall but lost when he disobeyed God's command. But Adam's desire to regain this position of proper authority is twisted now, resulting in an obsessive concern for

[79]

position, rights, status and authority.

After the Fall, Eve was also unable to exercise proper authority and accountability in marriage. Her obsessive desire was to regain lost community at any cost, which made her prone to subservience. Fear of separation dominates her relationships. She wants peace at any price. Her nostalgia for lost harmony in relationship becomes twisted for her into fallen social enmeshment. Where there should be mutual love and accountability, there is now dependency and dominance. Titles from some currently popular recovery books exemplify relationships governed by the fallen human nature: *Women Who Love Too Much, Why Do I Think I Am Nothing Without a Man? Men Who Hate Women and the Women Who Love Them.*

Men and women live in different worlds. This alienation has been with us since the Fall. We grow up learning to communicate within our own gender contexts. We learn best the language of our gender. We also appear to universally have the confusing experience of being terribly misunderstood when communicating with the opposite sex. Communication patterns that come naturally and work well for us in our own gender context often fail miserably outside that world.

Tannen describes these differences, which are rooted in scriptural events, from her perspective of modern research and observation. Women speak and hear a language of connection and intimacy, while men speak and hear a language of status and independence. This is why she says communication between the genders is crosscultural. Instead of saying we speak different dialects, Tannen says we speak different "genderlects."

Tannen believes men tend to see the world through a hierarchical grid. A man's world is predominantly an authoritarian social order. Men are often overly concerned with position, with who is up and who is down. Conversations and communications in a man's world are generally negotiations that focus on status and are energized by competition.

For men, life is a contest—a struggle to preserve independence and avoid failure, which can inhibit upward mobility. Men want relationships like women do, but they do not focus on these relational goals. They tend to pursue them primarily through competition. It is in contest and even conflict that men gain appreciation for one another and the mutual respect that can foster a relationship.

Women see the world as individuals existing in a network of connections, organized according to bad, good, better or best relationships. Levels of friendship and intimacy, not of power and authority, characterize this network. For women, the purpose of conversation is to negotiate closeness, with the goal of reaching unity. Life is a community, a struggle to preserve intimacy and avoid isolation. Women are also concerned with achievement, position in life and avoiding failure, but generally they are not as intensely focused on these as men. Women pursue achievement and position through a communication style of relational connection and intimacy.[2]

When Josh's old high-school buddy called him at work and announced he'd be in town on business the following week, Josh invited him to stay for the weekend. Later he informed his wife, Linda, that they would be having a houseguest for the weekend. Josh also announced that he and his friend would be going out together that Friday night to catch up with each other's lives.

Linda was upset. She was going away on business for several days, and that Friday night would be her first opportunity to see Josh. But she was most upset that Josh merely informed her of these plans after the fact, without discussing it together beforehand.

Their argument went this way. Josh said, "I can't say to my friend, 'I'll call you back, I have to check with my wife first.' " To Josh, checking means seeking permission, which implies he is not independent, not free to act on his own. This would embarrass him in front of his friend. It would make him feel like a child or an underling. But to Linda, checking with Josh on something has nothing to do with seeking permission or jockeying for position. She comes from a different world, a world where discussing plans together is a natural interchange between two people whose lives are intimately intertwined. She likes to say to her friends, "I have to check with Josh." It shows her friends that she is involved with someone, that her life is meaningfully connected with the life of another.

Linda was hurt because she interpreted the incident to mean that she and Josh were not as close as she thought. He obviously didn't care about her as much as she cared about him. Josh was hurt and confused because he felt she was trying to control him, to put him in an inferior position, and that she was insensitive to how this would embarrass him in front of his old friend. Both Josh and Linda were hurt in this incident because they did not understand the gender realities that operate in the normal world of the other person.[3]

This same kind of misunderstanding occurred between Louise and Harry. Harry buys whatever he wants, when he wants, without consulting Louise. Louise, on the other hand, would not think of buying anything major without talking to Harry first. Louise is upset about this, not because they can't afford the purchases, but because she feels degraded. His independent buying pattern signals to Louise that she's not as important to Harry as she thought she was.

This is another example of the difference between a man's world and a woman's world. In Harry's world, the concern is status. A man's level of independence is a sign of his status. Many women would consult with their partners before making major purchases because they appreciate the process of involvement in making decisions by consensus. But men feel oppressed by long discussions about what they see as relatively unimportant decisions. The problem is that the focal point for men is the decision, while for women it's the process. When a woman asks, "What do you think?" it is an invitation to discussion, a posture meant to emphasize the importance of the relational connection that exists. Men hear that question as asking for a decision to be made.[4]

Another common problem that can be understood by thinking about these gender differences is nagging. Women are simply more inclined to do what others request of them without feeling like they are being put down or that someone is jockeying for position. Women will ignore concerns about whether a request positions them up or down because maintaining the relationship is the highest priority.

Men, on the other hand, can be very sensitive to their position when they are requested to do something. They tend to resist any hint of someone telling them what to do. If a man's wife asks him to do something, he will often try to find a way to do what is requested while maintaining his independence. He may wait a while and then do it. Or he might do it right away, but in his own way, not the way suggested.

If the man does not respond immediately, his wife will probably think he just doesn't understand what she wants. If anyone asked her to do this simple thing she would do it immediately without even thinking about it. So the wife repeats the request. Now the husband's resistance increases. He feels pressured. He delays further or gets more obstinate about how the thing will be done. This vicious cycle results in continued nagging by the wife and increased stubbornness from the husband.

Another gender difference that Tannen mentions is how women commonly respond to other women's troubles by sharing troubles of their own or by connecting with sympathetic responses. Feelings are mutually affirmed. For men, the offering of sympathy can sound condescending. When someone at work offers sympathy, men often filter this through the grid of status. The message is "I'm so sorry that happened to you, Fred." But Fred hears, "You failed, Fred. You may not survive this. You have this problem or weakness." Also, when someone shares a problem or concern in a man's world, it is usually a bid for action, for decision-making. Men try

[83]

to solve the problem. This problem solving can be totally innocent, a genuine desire to help, but it is not usually what women are really looking for when they share a problem. A solution is an objective response to the words shared. But the underlying message a woman is hearing when a man offers a solution is that the man is minimizing her feelings. What a woman really wants to hear is something like "I know how lousy that has to feel," or a similar complaint, "Somebody did that to me and I felt the same way."

Women become frustrated when they don't get this reinforcement. They feel distanced by the advice men give. The underlying message they hear in male advice is "We're not the same. You have problems. I have solutions." When women share problems they are usually looking for an expression of mutual understanding. When men try to reassure women that their situation is not so bleak as it may seem, women hear their feelings being discounted or belittled.[5]

It's important to recognize that there is usually no malicious intent in the miscommunications between men and women. The man may be giving what he thinks the woman is asking for, and this is his way of expressing concern. He simply needs to understand what she really wants from him and isn't getting. He can learn this. And a woman can learn the elements of a man's world that contribute to his style of communication behavior so that she will not be hurt by reading into his statements things that are not there. She can also learn what he needs and communicate to him in a style that supports and encourages him in ways he understands.

When we step into and walk around in one another's world, we will be able to hear each other better. And we will learn to express ourselves in ways our partners can understand.

Questions for Discussion

1. Summarize the author's argument that the differences that

can lead to misunderstandings between men and women are rooted in the Genesis Fall.

2. Do you agree that men seem to be focused more on concerns about position and independence, while women appear to be more concerned for relationships and intimacy? Discuss.

3. Of the examples given, which situations of miscommunication between men and women are typical in your marriage relationship? How has the chapter helped you to understand better how simple conversations between spouses can go wrong?

4. How can husbands and wives help each other understand and accept their differences in communication styles? If some couples in your group have dealt with this issue, ask them to explain how they are learning to accept and understand each other's differences.

6
Tempted to Neglect Speaking the Truth in Love

•

Some of the best and most succinct guidelines for reaching deeper levels of honest dialogue with each other in our families can be found by studying the Old Testament Proverbs. For example, Proverbs 10:11 says, "The mouth of the righteous is a fountain of life, but violence overwhelms the mouth of the wicked." Putting the words *wicked* and *violence* together suggests to me a posture of the heart and the natural impact of this posture on the communication process. The heart of the wicked person is dominated by selfishness. Violence is the means by which this heart attitude finds expression in human relationships. This violence can be explosive or subtly manipulative. But it is always a form of violence to seek one's own way without regard for the other person.

Violence in Communication
A number of years ago Judie and some good friends helped me to see a side of myself that might have remained hidden if they had not loved me enough to point out what they saw. Yes, I did express love, caring and gentleness in relationships—most of the time. But if I cared deeply about an issue, or believed strongly that some-

thing should go a certain way, and someone got in my way, I would turn into the classic manipulator. I am good with words. I can use words to get my own way. I can bring on the heat or do the subtle thing. But it is violence against others, pure and simple, no matter how you slice it.

One night one of my friends stopped me after a church committee meeting during which I had come on pretty strong with a member of the congregation. He helped me to see what I had done when he called me "Samurai Minister." He meant it in fun, but he made his point too. I was grateful for the opportunity to reflect on my communication style. I am still learning to recognize the times when I try to manipulate Judie or one of the kids. We cannot express love and violence at the same time. I want to address my family with a loving heart.

Any manipulation aimed at selfishly satisfying or protecting ourselves is an act of violence, not an act of love. When we try to get our own way using strategies like punishment, intimidation or coercion, or the more subtle methods of flattery, seduction and deceit, we are manipulating. Wickedness characterizes the heart centered only on itself. We reduce the other person to an object to be maneuvered, outwitted, bullied, used. We are indifferent to the other person's freedom to make honest choices, the other's identity and integrity. This kind of communication violence unjustly silences or diminishes the voice of the other person.

We carry out this kind of violence with others in many ways. We may manipulate others on the basis of our position. A parent says, "You do what I tell you. I'm your father [mother], and I know what's best for you." The wage earner in the family says, "I'm the one who's making the money to pay for this, so the discussion is over." The man who thinks of himself as the ruler of the house says, "That's the way things are. If you don't like it, that's just too bad." The loved one says, "I shouldn't have to ask you to do this. You should know how I feel without my having to tell you." Or, "You know how much I want this. I'll really be hurt if you refuse." We leave no room in these strategies for an honest response from the other person.

Another common way we misuse power in communication is when we make winning any dispute our highest goal. We can develop techniques like throwing temper tantrums to silence the other. Or we can simply monopolize the conversation, not letting the other person get a word in edgewise. We can meander and drift around the periphery of an issue in order to frustrate the process, or keep changing the subject to confuse the other person. Another effective strategy is to never back down, never admit you are wrong or might have made a mistake. If you feel your position endangered, you may just clam up and refuse to go on, or explode and leave. Disengagement is a very effective technique. The husband blows up, leaves the house and tears away in the car. He returns after two or three hours and acts as if nothing has happened.

Most of us have experienced a wide variety of manipulative communication techniques. Someone may ask questions that force us into a double bind, where any answer we give will nail us to the wall. Or they may employ humorous or sarcastic comments to "cut us down to size." Inducing guilt and playing the martyr are classic manipulation techniques that effectively stifle honest communication. Sinful practices such as filing away our grievances for future use, name-calling and putting the other down all shut down open lines of exchange. Even sulking and the silent treatment are methods of violence against the process of honest dialogue.

The other side of the proverb says "the mouth of the righteous is a fountain of life." The righteous person's heart is filled with the love of God. Lovers view the other person as someone to be respected and prized. The righteous person is not self-centered or interested in sitting in the seat of power, but desires shared power. The righteous lover wants to empower the other, knowing that this is both right in itself and the best way to establish an equally satisfying relationship. This kind of attitude breathes life into the relationship. Freedom is emphasized, not coercion and manipulation. Genuine dialogue encourages the kind of openness and honesty where full respect for the other's position, whether in agreement or disagreement, is assured.

If we really love, we will resist every impulse to coerce. Above all we will want others to honestly feel the freedom to be fully and really themselves when they are with us. It is life-giving to have another respect your need to be heard and understood. Open, honest dialogue is to a marriage and family what blood is to the body. If the flow of blood ceases, the body dies. When dialogue is blocked, love dies and resentment and hate are born. The measure of good relationships is the quality of dialogue that exists within them. But even dying relationships can be revived, for "the mouth of the righteous is a fountain of life."

Hearing with Our Heart and Mind

Proverbs 18:13 says, "He who answers before listening—that is his folly and shame." First there has to be good listening; then there can be good answering. Listening is a powerful way to affirm another in love. When we truly listen, we are essentially telling the other person, "There is nothing in the world more important to me right now than you."

True listening requires giving our full attention to the other person. That means hearing with our minds and hearts. It's not just waiting for her to hurry up and finish so I can say what I want to say. It's sincerely waiting for her to finish, to fully say what she wants to say. We need to take time to consider her words, to make sure we have accurately received her message. We can learn to help the other talk openly and without reserve.

The goal of communication is to enter the other person's world of meaning, to minister love in the other's world. This is a tangible way of cultivating our relationship. But this requires humility and self-denial. Here again the selfish heart will militate against this act of love. We will want to talk. We will want center stage. But in listening we lay ourselves aside for a time, concentrate on the other and invite self-disclosure so we can affirm the authentic person revealed. This is a blessing we give in love, a gift that builds the relationship.

Good listening is not just silence. We can be silent without really attending to what the other person says. I taught junior high in public school for several years and learned in that atmosphere of pandemonium how to shut out the world around me. I still go into this protective mode at times. Judie or one of the kids will be talking to me, and I don't respond. They have learned (out of kindness to me) to inject humor into the situation by counting the number of times they can ask me the same question before I realize someone is trying to get my attention. But it's not funny, not really. When I don't hear the requests and conversations of the people who are most important to me, I am not caring for them the way I want to.

Good listening demands careful attention with body, mind and heart. We give the wrong message when we look over the other person's shoulder, glance at our watch, yawn or rub our eyes. Good listening means engaging our minds and opening our hearts to the other. We need to keep an open mind and heart. You can easily fall into the pattern of thinking you know what your husband is going to say before he says it. *I know him so well,* you say to yourself. If we pretend to know what the other person is going to say before he or she has spoken it, we are not listening. We are asserting ourselves again. This arrogance kills the possibility of new life in the relationship. We have to listen with an open mind to hear the fresh perspective that is struggling to be revealed.

It is also the closed mind that protests, "Get to the point! What's the bottom line?" What if there is no point? What if there is no bottom line? Isn't it enough for you that the one you love wants to share her life with you? Sometimes we just need to talk. This is the way we make sense of our confusing world. When I feel like this, I need someone who will listen from the heart.

The most common complaint I hear in counseling couples is that the husband, or the wife, does not listen. It is almost always the other person who has the problem. So it is most rare to have someone come in and say, "I don't listen well to my husband/wife. Can you help me to learn to listen better?" If each partner will take the servant's posture and focus on hearing the other well, balance and reciprocity in hearing and sharing can be born in the relationship. A healthy relationship has to give ample opportunity for mutual listening and speaking.

A good listener learns how to draw the other out in a conversation. Some of our richest times of sharing come when Judie will start asking me questions about things that I believe, or what is making me happy, or what my dreams are about the future. As I begin talking she asks me about other things, and the meaning of life grows between us. Sometimes I have asked her about her childhood. What was her bedroom like when she was a child? What kind of work did she do as a teenager? What did she remember about her mother, who died of cancer when Judie was eleven? It amazes me that after thirty-three years of marriage there are still vast areas of personality and memory to be explored.

After we have learned good listening, we can answer more effectively. If Judie tells me that I have embarrassed her by correcting her in front of others, and I immediately tell her why I was right and she was wrong, I have not listened well. I have answered before listening. If I really heard her I would simply say, "I'm sorry." If she says she was hurt by being corrected in front of others, and I respond by saying, "Yes, but you hurt me just before that when you said _____ ," I have not listened well. I have answered before I really listened to her from my heart.

I don't like to feel as though I've done something wrong, so I try to justify my actions. I place the blame elsewhere. I defend myself. This is folly and shame. Instead, I need to apologize and listen with an open heart. How did I hurt you? Do I act this way often? Is there an issue to be resolved here? How might I have approached the situation in a way that would not have been hurtful or embarrassing to you? In this way we can give a gentle answer. Proverbs 15:1 says, "A gentle answer turns away wrath, but a harsh word stirs up anger."

The greatest test of communication in a marriage is how conflict is managed. The disagreements we face are neither good nor bad, but the way they are handled can be destructive or constructive. Disagreements happen in marriage—especially if you have been married for a while and can honestly tell each other how you really feel. It takes listening with great integrity to know what the real issue is between you. Good listening and good answering will help you to work out together what will be the right time to address the issue, after cooling off and gaining perspective, and not when both of you are dead tired at the end of a long day.

If anger needs to be expressed, find ways to let it out without becoming abusive to the other. We learn in Ephesians 4:26 that we can be angry, but we must be careful not to sin against the other. No hitting below the belt. At the same time, it's not fair for a boxer to wear his trunks up around his neck. It takes good listening and good answering to maintain a positive environment as you're working through something tough. Encourage one another. Praise each other for honesty when it occurs and for the courage to expose areas of deep feeling to the light.

Recently Judie and I both noticed something we do quite naturally and unconsciously when we argue. Invariably one of us will reach out to take the other by the hand. In the midst of what is sometimes a fairly heated dispute, we will find ourselves suddenly holding hands. Something in us refuses to let the momentary conflict separate us. The touch that occurs so naturally between us when a dispute arises serves as a powerful reminder that the issue at hand cannot be allowed to gain power over the steadfast, lifelong bond we share together in love. The moment we gain this perspective, anger gives way to a more gentle spirit. We are able to speak and listen with kindness.

Speaking the Truth in Love

Proverbs 12:22 says, "The LORD detests lying lips, but he delights in men who are truthful." Nothing will bring more strength and health into your relationship than honesty. Honesty in communication is more than just words. Honesty is first of all promises made and kept. A promise is a commitment to live out our good intentions. When we live up to our promises, our partner learns that we are dependable. Then trust grows in our relationship. Increased trust brings greater intimacy. As we speak the truth in love, we mature in Christlikeness (Eph 4:15). This maturation will be observed in our relationship as unconditional love, grace and forgiveness.

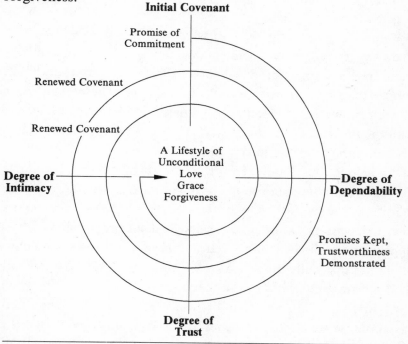

Figure 1. Loving in truth

Figure 1 shows how this process unfolds. Marriage rests on the initial covenant, the promised lifelong commitment. Dennis Guernsey and Ray Anderson explain what this means when they write, "It is covenant love that provided the basis for the family. For this reason, family means much more than consanguinity, where blood ties provide the only basis for belonging. Family is where you are loved unconditionally, and where you can count on that love even when you least deserve it."[1] The traditional marriage vows exhibit this kind of unconditional covenant. There are no conditions mentioned by which the marriage commitment can be dissolved.

Unfortunately, immature lovers make this promise with very little understanding of what it takes to live out. This is why we do premarital counseling—to dismantle unrealistic expectations and educate young men and women about the seriousness of the marriage covenant.

Young people have dreams of what their marriage will be like. They see a lifetime of unendending, unwavering romantic love with tireless energy for one another. They see the honeymoon cottage that somehow cleans itself twice a week. They have visions of perfect children, perfect work situations, perfect relationships with the in-laws. These unrealistic ideals can be like an infectious disease in the marriage relationship.

If you love your dream of a perfect marriage more than you love the real man or woman you married, your dream will destroy your marriage. The single most important attitude necessary for success in marriage is thinking honestly and realistically about the relationship from the beginning. But no amount of premarital counseling can ever fully prepare a couple for what it takes to live out their marriage covenant over a lifetime.

At first we freely trust our spouse. We believe what the other says because we choose to believe it in love. But this blind trust is a honeymoon stage that will soon require the evidence of dependable behavior. It is not the *words* of promise that build trust in a marriage, but *actions* based on that promise. The degree to which we keep our promises, demonstrate trustworthiness and act dependably determines the growth of trust in our relationships.

The promise wagers the relationship into the future. Hope and stability in the marriage are created through the power of our promises in the face of the uncertainties that lie ahead. This is why it is so important to make our promises carefully and to be promise keepers.

Unkept promises destroy trust. Uncertainty and doubt take the place of confidence and hope, essential elements of covenant relationship. Trust can be rebuilt, but only when we demonstrate trustworthiness. The amount of trust lost in a broken promise will be commensurate to how foundational the particular promise has been to the health of the marriage. A promise to be home from work at a certain time on a certain day, if broken once or even occasionally, will not make a serious dent in the level of trust in your relationship (especially if you have been making regular dependability deposits to your marriage safe-deposit box). But if your broken promise strikes at the core of what it means to be husband and wife together, forgiveness will be difficult, and future trust will be built slowly and with great effort.

The most destructive tearing of the fabric of trust comes if the marriage bed is defiled. No one who has made a covenant vow of faithfulness to another person has the right to experience sex outside of the parameters created by the marriage vows sworn under God. Walter Wangerin puts this well when he writes,

> The marriage vow subordinates one's individual satisfactions in all areas to one's marital partner—declaring publicly that sex is less important than one's spouse, less important than the health of the relationship. Sexual satisfaction is no longer a right, but a *blessing, a gift of the relationship* to its partners. This attitude, then—that the health of the relationship is infinitely more important than one's own desires, and that the sweet fulfillment of one's desires is an undeserving bounty within that relationship—not only closes the door to adulteries, but abolishes the door and the thought altogether.[2]

Be careful to preserve the trust in your relationship through de-

[95]

pendable behavior. Be a promise keeper. It is the only way to move on to the deeper levels of intimacy and love that can be ours in Christ.

Looking again at figure 1, we see that as trust grows, a couple can risk greater intimacy and honesty with one another. This is what it means to love in truth. As we reveal more of ourselves—the real self we've been afraid to show—and our partner receives us as we really are, we experience unconditional love. This is the most powerfully affirming human experience we will ever have. To be truly known and accepted is very rare indeed.

Judie demonstrates her love for me by willingly renewing her initial covenant with me each time she learns more about the real man she married. Each time she demonstrates her covenant commitment, even when discovering unpleasant aspects of my real self, I trust her more and am willing to risk greater intimacy.

This mutual process of greater knowing, loving and trusting allows us to experience in greater depth the promised "one flesh" in our marriage. At each stage of discovery we renew our commitment. This does not have to be formal. In fact, usually we simply go on with our spouse. But the "going on" demonstrates our continuing commitment to the relationship. Our selfish desires are increasingly swallowed up in love, grace and forgiveness. There is nothing more rewarding in life than to be able to speak the truth in love without fear. In this kind of honest marriage we are loved unconditionally, and we learn that we can count on that love even when we least deserve it.

The proverb says, "The LORD detests lying lips." Exactly what is a lie? A lie is an attempt to control reality for some selfish end. Either we want something to happen for us or we do not want something to happen to us, so we lie. Sometimes we lie to put off having to do the right thing. We promise to do something without ever intending to follow up. This is how a promise becomes a lie. Often we follow the broken promise with another lie. "Did I say that? I can't remember telling you that!" Or "Is that what you heard? That's not really what I intended." Lies chip away at dependability, which in turn destroys trust and inhibits intimacy in our marriage. God detests lying but takes delight in truthfulness. He will bless our marriages as truth prevails.

We may sometimes be tempted to flatter our spouse. Flattery distorts the truth in order to make the other person more responsive to our wishes. We don't need flattery. We need to trust the other person to be honest. But we need to be careful here. A commitment to honesty does not give us license to mock or criticize the other person. In our marriages we will want to major on honest praise and encouragement. Paul writes, "Do not let any unwholesome talk come out of your mouths, but only what is helpful for building others up according to their needs, that it may benefit those who listen" (Eph 4:29).

We should be eager to catch our wives or husbands doing something good so we can honestly praise them. Tell your husband when he pleases you. Tell your wife when you're proud of her. Honest praise is a gift that keeps on giving. Genuine, loving dialogue requires a steady diet of affirmation. We need to communicate regularly, authentically, honestly and in no uncertain terms that we prize the other person.

In this environment of mutual respect and honor, intimacy will deepen. We can trust someone who proves on a daily basis that he or she honestly has our best interests at heart. Authentic praise will strengthen your relationship and encourage mutual dialogue.

Questions for Discussion

1. Discuss what you believe the author means by "violence" in communication.

2. In what family situations might you be tempted to use a violent method that hinders communication? How might other family members answer this question for you?

3. Why might a person fear open and honest dialogue in the family?

[97]

4. Why do you think good listening is powerful in healthy communication? Why is it hard to be a good listener?

5. What are some practical strategies you might use to make sure you are listening well to your spouse or children? Have couples who believe they have been learning to listen to one another better explain what is working for them. How do they make sure they are hearing what each other is really saying?

6. The Bible says we can experience honest anger, but we are not to let it lead us into sin (Eph 4:26). Discuss how honest anger can be shared in a healthy manner in family relationships.

7. Why is keeping our promises vital in family relationships?

8. Discuss the meaning of the statement the author makes on page 94: "If you love your dream of a perfect marriage more than you love the real man or woman you married, your dream will destroy your marriage."

7

Tempted to Lose
Our Family
Closeness

•

In the last few years, Judie and I and our youngest
son, Gabe, have gone through a really rough time together. After
our move to California, we were happy that Gabe found some new
friends in junior high. They shared a lot of the same interests:
computers and computer games, sports, stereo systems, cars and
exploring in the hills near our home. We were glad for the friendships, but also worried because a few of the boys had some rough
edges, like bad-mouthing their parents and occasionally suggesting
activities that were really dangerous or could get them in trouble.
We were also troubled that there was often no supervision at the
other boys' homes.

In the beginning we told Gabe about our concerns, but said we
understood how important the friendships were to him. Gabe said
the other kids' parents told him he was a good influence on their
boys. The parents also told us how much they liked Gabe. We
continued to give Gabe freedom in the relationships but monitored
things fairly closely.

Near the end of Gabe's freshman year, things got worse. Gabe
would often come home smelling of smoke, although he claimed
he was not smoking. His circle of friends had grown larger, and

the new kids only increased our concern. Gabe even admitted that some of the boys were into drugs and drinking.

I remember going shopping with Gabe one afternoon and stopping at a restaurant for a cold drink. I told Gabe I was worried he might soon find himself in over his head with things he couldn't control. He assured me that he was not smoking and not interested in drinking or drugs. He liked the guys because they knew a lot about auto mechanics and he was learning about cars from them. As our conversation ended, I warned him that if things got out of hand, he would have to say no to these friendships. He said he understood.

About two months after that conversation Gabe came in one night smelling terribly of smoke. I had already gone to bed. Judie confronted Gabe, and he admitted that he had started smoking. The next day we sat down to talk again. I asked him not to spend any time with the other boys for a couple of weeks while the three of us thought through what would be the best thing to do. I remember looking at him as he sat in the chair next to the bed, and I started to cry because I was so worried for him. I tried to express what I was feeling, but only wound up saying, "You know how much I love you, don't you, Gabe?" He said he was sorry, got up, came over and gave me a hug. With his arms around me, he said, "I'll do whatever you say."

Things seemed to be going well for another month or two. Then one night Gabe stayed out past the time we had asked him to come home. It got later and later. Finally Judie decided to walk down the street where one of the boys lived to see if Gabe was there. The house was dark. She stood outside for a few minutes and then turned to come home. She was halfway home when Gabe came up beside her; he said he had seen her through the front window. She smelled marijuana on Gabe.

Gabe came home and went to bed. Judie and I stayed up talking and praying. I was well aware of how these tough decisions always have the potential to either heal or hurt a relationship. We were sure about what we had to do. We prayed that Gabe would be able to hear us.

The next day we drove to our church fall conference for the afternoon. Gabe's brothers did not want to go. We told Gabe we wanted him to come along because we needed to talk. At the conference grounds we were able to get away together, just the three of us. Judie and I told Gabe that the boys he had been spending time with for two years were no longer his friends. We reminded him of things he already knew about our past, that we both had struggled with drugs and alcohol during the sixties and that these things had nearly ruined our lives and our marriage. We told him we loved him too much to let him get swallowed up at his young age in alcohol and drug addiction.

At this point Gabe started to cry. He cried quietly for several minutes. Judie and I let him cry and said nothing. I did not know why he was crying. I thought it was probably because he was very angry at me for telling him he would no longer be allowed to spend time with his best friends. After he quieted down and relaxed, I asked him why he was crying. He simply said, "Because I was just thinking of how I might have ended up."

During his junior year things went very well for Gabe. He made the junior varsity basketball team and had a great year. He made some new friends from the team. His grades improved, and he was on the honor roll for the first time in his life. We were very hopeful and thankful, but as parents we both knew that Gabe's life could still go either way. Once a young person has opened the door to drugs and alcohol they live in a danger zone for a number of years until they mature to the point of being able to manage these temptations.

It was just after the first quarter of his senior year that Gabe got in trouble again. He was caught at his place of work selling beer and liquor to underage friends. This incident thrust Gabe into the legal system and a tangled mess that lasted most of his senior year and ended up with Gabe being on probation for six months after graduation. As hard as this time was, it was an important learning experience for all of us. Judie and I learned during the process that Gabe's drinking situation was worse than we had thought. When we believed he was doing so well, he had only gotten very good at covering it up. In counseling, Gabe was finally able to tell us about the enormous struggles he had been facing.

Through this period we stuck together as a family. I remember one family mealtime when we were all hurting with Gabe over some of the things he was having to go through in court. Gabe's brother Josh turned to him and said, "Gabe, you need to know that there is nothing you could ever do that could make us stop loving you. There is nothing any of us could ever do that would stop us from being a family. You will always be one of the brothers, Gabe, no matter what."

Gabe and I have talked about whether to include any of this in the book. One of the things we learned was how much pressure there always was on Gabe and the other kids to live up to being the pastor's kids. I have been worried about including this account because I do not want to put any more pressure on him. But Gabe felt he wanted to say some things that he believed would be helpful to other kids and parents. He wrote a long letter to Judie and me about our family, our parenting and other things he's learned. I'll share some of his insights here. Our prayer is that others can learn from the things we have gone through together.

About drugs and alcohol Gabe wrote,

The best advice I would give kids is that drugs are going to be around you all the time, even as early as junior high. You just have to learn to be strong and say "no." If your friends keep the pressure on you, there are plenty of other kids out there that also don't want to do drugs and drink that you can hang out with. If you're already involved with drugs and alcohol, get out of the trap before it's too late. Drugs like pot will lead to other drugs like cocaine, shrums, acid, etc. You will wreck your entire life if you can't get out.

Gabe also had some things to say about friends who put pressure on kids to do things like steal for them or sell them alcohol when it's against the law. He says, "It's not worth it. Your friends will tempt you to do it and leave you in the end. They'll always leave you in the end. You will only be left with your family and that judge you're looking at right in front of you."

On how Gabe felt about our parenting and some of the pressures he was under, he writes,

I think the hardest thing for me was to have to live up to this high standard. My dad was a minister. He would always compliment us on what good children we were and how good everyone else always thought we were. It seemed like I had to be the perfect kid. I couldn't do anything wrong. After a while I just couldn't stand it anymore. I just had to let go. I wanted to lead a different life than I was leading, something more exciting. That's why I turned to the drugs and alcohol. It seemed like a fun thing to do. I had no idea what it would lead to in later years. Other than that, the parenting was great. The main thing that got me through all of this was the love I got from my parents. Both of you always reminded me that whatever I did in my life there would be no way you wouldn't love me. I want to encourage my children in whatever they do, and always give them that special love.

Family Closeness

Through the tough times we shared with Gabe, and through many other difficult times we as a family have had to face together (and continue to wrestle with), our family closeness has kept open the channels of communication. This has bound our family together in times of crisis. All four of our children are out of the house now, living on their own, working and going to school. The only thing that has changed in our family communication is that it now costs us money to talk long-distance. We spend a lot of time on the phone.

[103]

Studies have shown that family closeness is a major factor in determining how individuals within the family face the temptations and struggles of modern life. Merton and Irene Strommen write,

> Family closeness actually fortifies children with an inner resistance to the toxins of life. The adolescent-parent study [that the Strommens conducted] shows that adolescents in a close family unit are the ones most likely to say "no" to drug use, pre-marital sexual activity, and other antisocial and alienating behaviors. They are also the ones most likely to adopt high moral standards, develop the ability to make and keep friends, embrace a religious faith, and involve themselves in helping activities. All of these characteristics pertaining to adolescents from close families are significant—which means that the evidence cannot be attributed to mere chance.[1]

The Strommens' study also shows that the *desire* to communicate in families remains high through upper elementary school and into adolescence, but the *ability* to communicate steadily decreases. There are a number of reasons this is true. During this time parents need to be conscious of the changes taking place in their kids. If family closeness remains a high priority, being sensitive to these changes will help you keep communication flowing through all the difficult transitions you will face with your kids.

Kids enter adolescence with a growing insecurity about who they are. They become hypersensitive about themselves as they grow toward adulthood. As parents we need to recognize that they will be easily hurt, often devastated, by criticism, especially in front of their friends. We should live by the adage "Affirm in public, correct in private." Major on affirmation and confront your kids only when it's really necessary. We need to let go of many things that just don't matter all that much. Honest and open dialogue with our kids is far more important than if they eat all their green beans. If correction is needed, a less authoritarian posture should be communicated. Talk to your adolescent kids as you would talk to a coworker, with gentleness, respect and sensitivity. Do far more listening than talking.

We should also remember that young men and women often lack the mature verbal skills necessary to freely express what they are going through. Self-expression seems particularly difficult for boys. Parents who really want to keep in touch at this stage will have to make quantity time a priority—time just to "be with" your kids without a hidden agenda. Patience and a relaxed atmosphere will often allow communication to happen naturally. If we find ourselves snatching quick moments here or there to talk, genuine communication will rarely take place. Having relaxed, nonthreatening times together keeps the dimensions of friendship alive between parents and kids. When a crisis does arise, we are better prepared to handle it because it occurs in the midst of an ongoing and deepening relationship.

All of our kids have been very different. It is important for us as parents to find the best ways to communicate with each individual in the family. Jana, our oldest, hits things head-on and strikes while the iron is hot. Josh talks most freely with his mom or me when we get him off alone. Jason is very up-front and will respond honestly to questions we ask. He is easy to talk with. Gabe has always been quieter and does a lot of internal processing. Gabe and I can ride together in the car for fifteen minutes without saying anything to each other. Sometimes I can get him going with a question or two, but often this doesn't work. I'll get a short answer followed by a long silence. This really doesn't bother me or him. We can feel good being together without having to talk all the time.

In the middle of a major argument with Gabe, I stumbled upon a new way for us to understand each other. At the time we were both so angry that I thought it best to wait and let things cool down. So later I wrote down a few sentences about what I was feeling and put them on his pillow. The next morning I had a three-page letter on my dresser. After he had carefully thought things through and wrote them down, we got together and talked through our disagreement.

This exchange of intrahousehold mail with Gabe also taught me another important part of adolescence. Teenagers want to make more of their own decisions without our help. As our kids mature, we need to make sure that we talk with them on more of a peer level. We need to treat our adolescent sons and daughters with respect, not as children under our authority. This kind of sensitivity reduces emotional distance and breaks down defenses between family members.

Little things like guarding our tone of voice when making a request or offering a suggestion can make a huge difference. Saying "*I want* you to do this" in an authoritarian manner can make sensitive kids feel humiliated, not recognized as persons. Think instead how different this might sound: "Would you please help me with this?" "It would help me a lot if you could do this." Simple politeness shows respect.

Kids whose parents treat them with respect and acknowledge their growing maturity, regardless of age, will often think of their parents as friends. Even the youngest children blossom when we speak to them without condescension, as people whose opinions and ideas are worth listening to.

Our authoritarian stance often becomes stronger as the kids grow up and we feel our authority slipping away. I am not suggesting by this that we give up our role and position as parents and turn things over to the kids. But we have to fight the tendency to come on too strong. We need to recognize that our kids are going through a natural and necessary process of growing into adulthood.

Practical Ways to Stay Close
Try to create and protect family times that allow for good dialogue to take place. I especially enjoy driving on long trips when there is nothing to do for hours but chat with each other. As often as

possible Judie and I try to get away with each of the kids alone. We have done family mission trips together which create tremendous times of interaction. Judie and I have also each done short-term mission trips and other brief vacations where we have taken one child with us. These times create rich interaction in an unusual setting where you relate to one another differently from the way you would at home. I also like to take one of the kids with me when I go on a speaking trip. They hear and see me in a different setting and are likely to ask me questions later about some of the content and personal things I've shared. These times together all build the family closeness we want.

We had some good success with a weekly family Bible study time when the boys were in high school. We set aside an hour to discuss a brief passage of Scripture and how it related to our lives. These times always opened up interesting family sharing. Judie and I were often amazed at how much our kids were thinking about.

Try to preserve even brief times together, like suppertime. Studies on family life suggest that there is a strong relationship between the feelings and memories of love in the home and mealtimes shared together as a family. When Josh called us recently he said this very thing. What he misses most now that he is living away from home is the family closeness we shared around the evening meal.

As our kids get older, these family times provide great opportunities for parents to be more vulnerable about their personal struggles. Our kids often grow up thinking we parents are really together individuals. We rightly protect our kids from many of the pressures of life. But as they mature, it's appropriate and healthy for them to know about the more personal side of our lives. Be honest when you are angry, hurt or confused. Denying your true emotions only hinders family communication.

We especially try to cover up angry emotions rather than admit them and deal with them. A mother may respond in anger at her daughter, but then quickly adds, "Sorry, I didn't sleep well last night." If that's not the true source of her anger, then she has interacted in an emotionally dishonest and unhealthy way. At those times when I feel let down in some significant way, or when I fail Judie or one of the kids, I am unable to hold back my tears. If we share our emotions honestly, our children will be able to relate to us as real persons rather than some unrealistic image we project.

Our children will be glad to learn that the struggles they experience are not that different from the problems we face. When they see you make it through tough times, it gives them hope that they can live with their struggles and still be effective in life. It also creates a strong bond of mutual understanding between parents and kids.

Don't be afraid to ask your children for advice—what they think you should do or how you should handle something. Some parents worry about confusing their kids, or that including them in important family decisions might undermine parental authority. But your kids can bring fresh insight into your life. Allow correction to go both ways. Learn from your children. Admit when you're wrong. Don't be defensive. Maintain a sense of good humor about yourself. The posture we assume in talking to our kids may be one they adopt when they need to discuss something important with us.

Learn to enter into the world of your kids if you really want to communicate. Be willing to focus more on their lives and concerns. Parents often give the impression that the things most important to their children are just silly, or kids' stuff. But what appears trivial to us may be all-important to our children. If a child is devastated by a small, hurtful comment from a friend, what is accomplished by our saying something like "Why are you worrying about *that?*" We need to see the difficulties our children face in their world from their vantage point. We should treat their struggles with the same seriousness that they do. Otherwise we make it difficult to keep the lines of communication open.

Pray for Your Family Communication

Prayer can bring deep healing to faulty family communication patterns. When a situation looks hopeless, when the walls between you appear formidable, God can, and often will, miraculously change attitudes and circumstances so communication will flow freely again.

We live in a world of complex problems. On top of that, we are sinful, selfish and stubborn people. Often it takes the power of God to break through the walls that have grown up between us as husbands and wives, and as parents and children.

Family communication works on a "loaves and fishes" economy. Jesus once fed a crowd of five thousand on five barley loaves and two small fish. Our families hunger for healthy, loving dialogue. Our needs are great and our human resources always inadequate. But rather than focusing on what we lack, we need to bring what little we have to Jesus. He will multiply our resources until they are sufficient to meet the need. We can trust him to do this.

Ask God to use your communication skills to further his kingdom within your family. Honestly confess before God your desire to communicate with one another more effectively. You may be surprised at how God will satisfy your longing. Only in Christ can you begin with a few loaves and fishes and end up with twelve baskets of love overflowing.

Questions for Discussion

1. How close do you think you are as a family? How do you measure your family closeness? What are the signs that tell you whether you are a close family or not?

2. What are some of the reasons that family communication gets tougher as children enter adolescence? What can parents do to try to make this transition easier?

3. In your family do you practice the rule "Affirm in public, correct in private"? Why would this be a good rule for kids and couples to follow?

4. Talk about what you're learning regarding how each child's communication style is a little different. How would you describe the characteristic communication style of each of your individual children?

5. What ideas from this chapter can help you to improve your family closeness?

6. The author believes that as children mature, it is healthy for parents to be more open and vulnerable about their personal struggles, and that older children should be included in the decision-making process when the parents and family are facing difficult times. Describe what you believe is a healthy balance in this area.

8
Tempted to Misunderstand Family Leadership

•

Judie and I were visiting once with a Christian woman who had been married only a few months. She was already upset about her new husband's deficiencies in the area of family leadership. She believed that the man had authority over the wife, and the wife was to submit to her husband. Judie and I both thought it was ironic and humorous when she told us vehemently, "I'm going to teach him to be the head of the house if it's the last thing I do."

Most of the discussions in Christian circles about family leadership are attempts to understand how key biblical principles inform the dynamic interplay of authority and love in the "one flesh" organism we call marriage. The differing positions that Christians hold regarding the roles of men and women in marriage often lean one way or another based on how certain key words are interpreted in the apostle Paul's well-known passage on marriage, Ephesians 5:21-33. Earnest Christians differ widely in the way they interpret and respond to concepts that Paul weaves through this passage, concepts like *headship, submission* and *agape love*. We will take a closer look at the Ephesians passage once we have considered what Jesus has to say in general about leadership in the kingdom of God.

Jesus' Style of Kingdom Leadership

James and John came to Jesus requesting that he allow them to sit at his right and left hands when he achieved his glory (Mk 10:35-45). The other disciples were angered by the request. Each one seemed secretly convinced that he was a cut above the others. They had even been arguing among themselves about who was the greatest (Mk 9:34). Jesus called them together like a father gathering his children and made this striking comparison between the way of the world and the way of the kingdom:

> You know that those who are regarded as rulers of the Gentiles lord it over them, and their high officials exercise authority over them. Not so with you. Instead, whoever wants to become great among you must be your servant, and whoever wants to be first must be slave of all. For even the Son of Man did not come to be served, but to serve, and to give his life as a ransom for many. (Mk 10:42-45)

Jesus says that kingdom leadership is not demonstrated by title or rule, dominance or control, but by sacrificial love. In the kingdom of God, those who love first and foremost are true leaders. God's leaders willingly give up their self-centered concerns for the good of others. Kingdom leaders give of themselves in costly service, patterned after the Lord Jesus Christ, our Master, who paid love's ultimate price. Because he is Lord of the kingdom, Jesus' definition of proper kingdom authority is foundational to all discussions about leadership.

At family conferences I have often addressed the topic of gender roles in marriage, beginning with this same story in the life of Jesus. On occasion a man will raise his hand in frustration and say, "Let's get to the point. Who's the head of the house? What does the Bible say?"

As I see it, a Christian man should not be asking that question, at least not in that way. Christians are not concerned about who's the boss. They should not spend their time like the disciples, arguing about who is the greatest or the most powerful. Instead

Christian men and women are interested in how their lives can reflect the attitudes and behaviors of their Lord. They're concerned with how they can lay down their lives for one another in love and service.

In Ephesians 5:21-33, the apostle Paul presents a radical new model for Christian marriage. A translation incorporating some helpful nuances present in the Greek text reads like this:

21Because you revere Christ, subordinate yourselves to one another—22wives to your husbands—as to the Lord. 23For [only] in the same way that Christ is the head of the church—he, the savior of his body—is the husband the head of his wife. 24The difference notwithstanding, just as the church subordinates herself [only] to the Messiah, so wives to your husbands—in everything.

25Husbands, love your wives, just as [we confess] Christ has loved the church and has given himself for her 26to make her holy by [his] word and cleansing her by the washing with water, 27to present her to himself as a radiant church, free from spot or wrinkle or any other blemish so that she may be holy and blameless.

28In the same manner husbands also ought to love their wives, for they are their bodies. In loving his wife a man loves himself. 29For no one ever hates his own body, but he provides and cares for it—just as Christ does for the church 30because we are members of his body. 31"For this reason a man will leave his father and mother and be joined to his wife, and the two become one flesh." 32This [passage] holds a profound mystery: but I am talking about Christ and the church. 33In any case, one by one, each one of you must love his wife as himself, and the wife . . . may she respect her husband.[1]

In Paul's day the relationship between Jewish husbands and wives was ordered according to the condition created by the Fall of Adam and Eve—"your husband will rule over you." Every morning a Jewish male gave thanks to God that he had not been made a

Gentile or a woman. Gentile husbands and wives, meanwhile, were likely to follow the pattern taught by Aristotle, "the courage of a man is shown in commanding, of a woman in obeying."[2] I believe that in this passage Paul challenges the church to a radically new kind of marriage relationship, one that ran directly counter to the social, religious and cultural biases of both Jews and Gentiles in his day.

First, Paul specifies for wives their part in the loving interaction of mutual submission in a marriage. He writes, "Wives, submit to your husbands as to the Lord. For the husband is the head of the wife as Christ is the head of the church, his body, of which he is the Savior" (vv. 22-23). Paul addresses the wives directly. If Paul had wanted to express this in the customary manner of his times he would have written instead, "Husbands, make your wives submit to you." But Paul addresses the women of the church as individuals capable of making their own decisions regarding such important matters as their style of relating in marriage.

Then in another radical shift from accepted practice, Paul asks wives to defer in love to their husbands—only their husbands, not to all men. In that culture women were expected to be subservient and obedient to all men. Paul's manner of speaking directly to the women in the church and then asking them to be submissive to their husbands alone would have been a challenging departure from conventional first-century cultural biases.

Paul's command for women to submit is defined and qualified by Christ's headship of the church. Paul writes, "For in the same way that Christ is the head of the church—he, the savior of his body—is the husband the head of the wife" (v. 23). Only in the same way as Christ is head of the body—that he would give his life to save her—is the husband the head of the wife. Christ loved the church so much that he would die for her, give his life for her, so that she could share in every heavenly blessing.

The word *head* as we use it in English can mean both the head of a person's body or, figuratively, the leader of an organization or group. We use the one word for either. In the Greek, however, there are two different words that can be used to express these concepts, *arche* and *kephale*.

Arche is commonly and consistently used in Scripture to suggest the first in power and position. We use the derivative prefix in English in words like *archangel* or *archbishop*. This use of *arche*, referring to those who rule in positions of power and authority, is variously translated in Scripture as "magistrate," "chief," "ruler," "prince" and "head." The term is also used in Scripture to express origin or first things. This aspect is picked up in the prefix of English words like *archetype* or *archaeology*.

If, in the Ephesians 5 passage, Paul had meant to convey the idea that the husband was to rule over his wife, *arche* would have been a perfect word for him to use. It would have been the perfect choice because that is the essential meaning of the Greek term as it is consistently used. Because *arche* can also be used to denote origin or source, Paul could have captured an excellent double meaning with the term, reminding his readers that in one sense Adam was the source of the woman. Both meanings of *arche* would have fit perfectly Paul's intentions, if this is what he had wanted to communicate.

Instead Paul chose to use the Greek term *kephale* to capture his intent. *Kephale* has as its first meaning the physical head of a body. *Kephale* can also be used to suggest authority, but it is a special kind of authority marked by agape love. Earlier in Ephesians Paul stresses the Lord's ruling position over the world and his headship of the church. He says God raised Christ and seated him at his right hand, "far above all rule *[arche]* and authority, power and dominion. . . . God placed all things under his feet and appointed him to be head *[kephale]* over everything for the church, which is his body, the fullness of him who fills everything in every way" (Eph 1:21-23). Paul refers to two kinds of authority in this passage. First he mentions the authority inherent in Christ's position "over *all things,*" and then he presents a second type of authority pictured by Christ's headship *in the church.*

The Lord holds a ruling position over principalities and powers. To emphasize this, Paul uses *arche* in verse 21 when he says Christ rules over all other "rule and authority." But his headship in the church is not pictured by Paul in the same way. If Paul wanted to emphasize the authoritative rule of Christ over the church, he would have used *arche.* But Paul uses *kephale* to express Jesus' headship in the church. Jesus is the "head" of his own body. Rather than using power imagery or emphasizing rule and command, Paul says instead that Jesus' headship is demonstrated by a continual filling of the body with the fullness of himself.

In other instances in ancient literature where *kephale* takes on the metaphorical meaning of authoritative position, it is consistently used in the unique sense of a capstone positioned to provide strength for a doorway, or a cornerstone positioned to bring stability to a building. It is significant that the word is never translated in the New Testament or the Septuagint (the Greek translation of the Old Testament) to mean "ruler," "chief" or "boss." Another way that *kephale* has been used to describe leadership is in a military context, but not the leadership of a captain or general who commands the troops from a position of safety behind the lines. Used in a military metaphor, *kephale* refers to the leader who goes before the troops, the leader who is the first one into battle.[3]

In the Ephesians 5 passage, Paul uses *kephale* throughout to maintain a consistent emphasis on the body concept. Paul obviously wants us to draw meaning from his parallel comparisons between the "one flesh" relationship of the man and woman in marriage and the oneness that is the unity of the church as one body, with Christ as head. The husband is the head of the wife, Paul says, in their one flesh bond, as Christ is the head of his body, the church. Christ became head of the church by giving himself up for her.

"Those who are regarded as rulers *[archein]* of the Gentiles lord it over them" (Mk 10:42). But this is not a Jesus-style headship, and it will not be the leadership style of the husband and father in the Christian family.

Paul focuses on the power of agape in headship, not on the power of rule and authority. Agape is totally selfless, other-centered love. It is the love that characterizes Christ's love of the Father and the love of God the Father for us. Husbands are to love their wives with this kind of relentless, tireless, self-giving love.

In the Ephesians 5 passage, Paul describes the husband's obligation in marriage as a willingness to give up his cultural right to dominate his wife. Instead he chooses to love her sacrificially. Paul's definition of headship here is active love and nurture, not control, dominance or oppression.

The submission of a wife to her husband is a submission of grace. The wife is asked to yield her selfish concerns, her rights and powers, to a husband who shows her every day that he loves her so much that he is willing to give up his life to make the marriage work. The wife is not being told here to be obedient to her husband. There is no New Testament verse that describes the relationship of the wife to the husband as one characterized by obedience.

John Stott describes the mutual submission in marriage this way: "Submission is something quite different from obedience. It is a voluntary self-giving to a lover whose responsibility is defined in terms of constructive care; it is love's response to love."[4] The yielding of the wife to her husband can be thought of as the action one senator might take in deferring to a fellow senator she deeply respects, or a soldier gladly joining the ranks of a leader who willingly risks his life to step out ahead of the rest as they go into battle together.

The men of Paul's day were predisposed by cultural norms and Greco-Roman and Jewish customs to view women as nothing more than property. The man was expected to demand, dominate, use women at will, even physically abuse and sexually mistreat women. Paul takes a giant leap forward in this passage. He tells men to submit their Jewish and pagan rights of position to their wives and to view the marriage relationship as a mutual interplay of sacrificial love and goodwill. Paul commands men to model the selfless love of Christ in their relationships to their wives and children.[5]

The Influence of a Loving Leader

Jesus is our model for family leadership. He used the power of love to empower others to be everything they could be. He empowered others to grow beyond their weaknesses so that they could manage their own lives under God. Jesus refused to take advantage of another's weaknesses for selfish ends. Instead he encouraged the development of strengths he saw in the men and women around him. He acted in the power of love to empower others to become loving leaders after his example.

Leadership is influence. What style of influence will we choose in our families? Will we try to manage others' lives through the power of dominance, or will we lead by the infectious influence of love? The headship that Paul describes in Ephesians, whether the headship of Christ in his body, the church, or the headship of the husband in the "one flesh" relationship of marriage, is empowerment. Biblical headship in marriage is an agape-style love that always looks to build up the other person and, by extension, the community.

If a man is to be head in the family community as Christ is head in the church, then he will make it his chief aim to encourage in love all family members, that they may reach the highest level of individual maturity possible. If the husband will model headship after the Christ model, he will be the first to recognize the gifts of others, especially those gifts beyond the scope of his own ability and personality. He will creatively facilitate the inclusion of these gifts in the working interaction of family life. He will demonstrate love and appreciation for the uniqueness of each individual in the family and will applaud and affirm the contributions others make. He will demonstrate his part in the dance of mutual submission in love by being quick to admit failure, quick to ask forgiveness, first in serving the family. These are the marks of strong leaders in the church and strong leaders in the family.

There is no dysfunction here. This leader does not demand submission from others, but willingly yields any rights to his selfish preferences with the view of lifting the family to greater health through the demonstration of Christlike love.

Every Family Member a Leader

A biblical conception of family life, and its community of relationships, must take into account the gifts God has given to the body of Christ. The church "grows and builds itself up in love, as each part does its work" (Eph 4:16). Every member of Christ's body has been gifted by God through the Holy Spirit and has a unique and significant contribution to make to the maturing community. In the same way, every member of our families has been gifted by God through the Holy Spirit and has a unique and significant contribution to make to the maturing family. This concept of giftedness applied to the family is what brings the greatest growth and health.

Kingdom leadership is the active influence of love. It is not dictatorship. Kingdom leadership is demonstrated by the loving empowerment of others. It is recognizing the gifts and abilities of others and empowering them to be everything they can be for Christ. This is how we influence the maturity and health of the community of faith. When individuals are growing in the use of their God-given gifts, everyone becomes a leader, influencing others in a positive way. Every family member, no matter what age or gender, has a significant contribution to make to the overall health of the family.

Judie and I talked again recently about how our individual children have contributed leadership in our family. Jana, our oldest daughter, has always been a strong model for the other kids of what it means to work hard around the home and in her studies and jobs. She is very caring in her relationships with others. But she has also had the courage to stop seeing boyfriends who did not treat her well, even though she loved them. This has been a good influence on her brothers. She has also been very accepting of people from different cultures, which has encouraged the whole family to be more open to those who are not exactly like us. Jana's independence, her work ethic, and her love and acceptance of a wide variety of people are leadership qualities that have been a strong influence in our family.

Joshua is very discerning about problems in the family and about moral issues and concerns in life. Josh would be the first to call a family meeting when we all lived together. Now that the three boys are living in an apartment, he still calls family meetings. Josh is also vulnerable in a healthy way about his own areas of struggle where he does not feel he is living up to what he professes to believe. His willingness to admit his problems and work to correct them is an encouragement to all of us. If Judie and I want to be held accountable in an area of growth, we know we can ask Josh as a young adult to give us a word of exhortation if he sees that we are not living the way we should. Josh is also a fine and caring best friend to many people. He is a model of a dependable and trustworthy friend.

Jason has a strong sense of justice and fairness. Jason will be the first to stand with someone who has been unfairly treated, even if it costs him. He did this all the way through school, and he still does this today among his friends and at work. He will speak the truth even if it gets him in trouble. His courage in this has been a strong influence on the rest of our lives. Jason also is an excellent manager of his own affairs. He is good at managing his money without being cheap (when he was younger he managed his candy in the same way). Jason is also a dependable friend.

Gabe is very sensitive and a good listener to anyone who is hurting. He is generous (we think sometimes to a fault, although his freedom in this area is a challenge to Judie and me). Gabe will be the first one to help someone move, go out in the middle of the night to talk with someone who needs a friend, or loan you some money (if he has any). Gabe is a gifted artist, but never calls any attention to himself, and mostly uses his artistic talents to create things he can give to others. He is also the most mechanically inclined person in the family. He helps keep the family cars and other mechanical things running. Gabe is trusting of others, which sometimes gets him into trouble, although his simple openness is a trait each of us wishes were more a part of our own character.

These characteristics revealed themselves in our children early on. We observed how they learned from each other and how we learned from them as our family grew up together. You might want to think about your children in this way. What would be missing in the family dynamic if one of your children had not been part of the family? What unique contribution does each person make to your family? How has each member of the family influenced the style of family leadership? This kind of reflection gives us a deeper appreciation for the special skills, dispositions and character traits that God has given to each member of the family.

Recognizing that God has gifted each person in the family community should radically alter the way we typically think about family leadership dynamics. Family life based on this charismatic (gifted) community model is not structured with the father as the ruler over subordinates, but with the father as team leader. The family works *together* to develop the strongest possible expression of Christ's self-sacrificial love and to offer that love to others. The Bible describes the "head" as the one who models selfless love and encourages all family members to develop their gifts to the fullest.

Paul singles out husbands for this teaching because the men of his day needed to hear this challenging word about the agape style of leadership. Many of us men today also need this challenge to lead our families in love. But this style of leading and modeling should not be the sole responsibility of the husband. Every member of the family can have a powerful and positive influence on every other member if each is encouraged to grow to a level of mature contribution. Then the family will be built up in love and strength as each part does its work.

Each family member—husband, wife, sons and daughters, grandparents, grandchildren—has distinctive God-given gifts, abilities and personalities to be deployed for the good of the family and the body of Christ. Each member of the family should be encouraged by other members to develop his or her unique gifts in the context of love. We can see that every family member is significant, each one needed, each perspective offering something to the completion and mature functioning of the whole. If these gifts are encouraged and flourish in the family, there will be health. If, instead, any family member dominates the others and refuses to allow them the opportunities to develop and use their gifts, then to the degree that individuals are inhibited, the health and maturity of the family will suffer.

Even in the best family there will still be creative tensions that have to be worked out. In the attempt to encourage each member's individual growth, there will be conflict. Often one member of the family will be encouraged to grow and develop while others sacrifice to make this happen. This is what it means to be willing to mutually submit to one another in love. Raising children requires this kind of sacrifice from parents. Mothers and fathers often have to give up things they would like to do for the sake of their children. A father may have to turn down an attractive promotion because he knows that this would be a bad time to make a family move. A mother who wants to finish her own college degree may have to postpone her education so that she can work to support her kids through college. A son or daughter selecting a college or university may need to accept a less expensive school to reduce the financial stress on the family. All these tensions can be worked out together in a family where individuals care enough to listen to each other and include each member in the decision-making process.

Dynamic Family Leadership
We affirm with Scripture that the husband is the head of the wife.

The husband has a unique position of initiation and influence in the family. His leadership, though, is not an influence of dominance, but the influence of sacrificial love. He is to fill the family with his care and love. The husband is the head of his wife and family as Christ is the head of the church.

We also affirm the scriptural teaching that the love relationship shared between the husband and wife is one of willing, mutual submission. The husband and wife in mutual submission to one another lead by example. Their model of shared leadership encourages family members to honor and serve one another as the family grows to maturity in love.

Every family member adds something to the leadership dynamic in the family structure. This does not mean that the family has more than one mother or father, or even more than one set of parents. Fathers and mothers, husbands and wives have responsibilities only they can fulfill in their families, and it is their obligation to fulfill their particular calling. But parents are not the only individuals in the family who provide leadership. Children are also uniquely gifted by God to influence the direction and health of our families. If we can grasp this concept, we will be less prone to erect artificial barriers in our families—barriers based on tradition or gender. We will be quick to recognize and encourage the unique gifts and callings of each family member. This is the way our families can be dynamically structured according to the scriptural model of the gifted community.

Have we sufficiently developed the place of spiritual authority in the family? I think so. Respected and trusted authority in any Christian context is always earned by the steadfast demonstration of Christlike humility and a willingness to give one's life for others in sacrificial love.

Questions for Discussion

1. What are the foundational qualities of kingdom leadership that Jesus taught his disciples in Mark 10:35-45?

2. The author believes that in Ephesians 5 the apostle Paul was offering a view of healthy relating in marriage that was radically different from the cultural view of his day, and far ahead of his time. What evidence is given to support this idea? Do you agree or disagree? Why?

3. Discuss the significance of Paul's use of the word *kephalē* rather than *archē* in Ephesians 5 to define an appropriate style of "headship" for the Christian man in a marriage relationship.

4. Leadership is influence. How does each member of your family uniquely influence the growth and health of your family community? How is each person providing some aspect of leadership in your family?

5. What would it look like for a husband to love his wife as Christ loved the church?

9
Tempted to Blur Boundaries

•

This past year the Mississippi River poured over its banks in one of the worst floods of the century. The water flowed into fields and towns, covered roads and highways and displaced thousands of families from their homes. The river spread its banks east and west, expanding its contour miles wide in some places. It looked more like a great lake than a great river.

I grew up on the Mississippi. I know what the river is supposed to look like. It is defined by its boundaries, the riverbanks. The river is a good thing if it stays within its boundaries. It is good for boating and fishing, barges carry grain and ore and coal from the northern states to the sea, crops are irrigated, electricity is generated, and river water is purified and used by millions who live along the Mississippi's banks.

I have also seen firsthand the devastation caused when the river floods. The powerful water washes over the riverbanks. When it does, the river becomes something altogether different. It is no longer safe. It cannot be trusted. When the Mississippi overflows its boundaries, it violates other boundaries like fields, towns, homes, businesses, parks and roadways. Flooded over with water, these things lose their identity. They are no longer able to function normally or serve their particular purpose. The violation of normal boundaries disrupts everything. Nothing remains intact. Life cannot go on with any sense of security.

A similar kind of trauma occurs when one person violates the boundaries of another person. Simply stated, our personal boundaries are emotional and physical fences, property lines, contours that define who we are in relation to others. Our most obvious physical boundary is our skin; our skin is the beginning of our physical self that separates who we are from who others are. The physical boundary of our body can be violated by others. We also have emotional boundaries. Our emotional boundaries can be violated as well.

Healthy, appropriate boundaries bring security and safety to our lives. If we have boundary problems, we will have a weakened sense of self. We will continually struggle to maintain proper control or to take responsibility for our lives.

Healthy boundaries help us to

1. identify, understand and accept who we really are in relation to others,

2. avoid violating someone else's space and controlling that person in an unhealthy manner,

3. keep other people from violating our space and controlling us in an unhealthy manner.

We all have to learn what boundaries work for us to achieve a sense of health and balance in our lives. And we need to learn to respect the boundaries of others. Our children need help to grow up with a healthy sense of boundaries, or they will struggle with self-esteem and issues of control in their adult lives. They also need to learn that other individuals live in this world and that their boundaries need to be respected.

In a healthy family everyone learns how to say yes to things that are right or good and no to things that are wrong or bad. In our relationships with others, we have to learn both how to *say* an appropriate yes or no and how to *hear* an appropriate yes or no.

[126]

Developing good boundaries for ourselves and respect for others brings security and trust into all of our relationships. If we can create and maintain healthy boundaries as parents—learning what we are and are not responsible for in our relationships with others—then we can help our children to understand how to manage their lives and relationships with self-awareness and confidence.

Summary of Typical Boundary Problems

In their book on boundaries, Henry Cloud and John Townsend suggest that there are four typical ways of blurring boundaries in our relationships. Those who exhibit these boundary problems in their personalities are called *Compliants, Controllers, Nonresponsives* or *Avoidants.*[1]

The *Compliant* says yes to things that are wrong, bad or unhealthy. Fear or false guilt dominates the compliant person's will. A compliant person is afraid to confront others to address a problem in a relationship. Compliants are also prone to take on too much reponsibility for the lives of others. The term *codependency* describes this blurring of boundaries. One woman joked that she found out she was hopelessly codependent when she fell into swift water one day and was drowning, and her husband's life flashed before her eyes. We have to learn that we are not responsible for the feelings, attitudes and behaviors of others.

Compliants also tend to become involved in abusive relationships. Their boundaries are so fuzzy that they allow abuse, often without recognizing what's happening to them. If they realize that they are in an abusive relationship, they find it hard to get out. It is as if their "no" has been disabled by fear. Compliants are afraid of hurting someone by saying no. They fear that their "no" will make the other person angry, or that they will be punished in some way, or will appear selfish. They don't want to rock the boat. But the price they pay is living under the control of another's demands.

The *Controller* does not respect the boundaries of others. Con-

[127]

trollers can't hear "no." They are always on the lookout for others who will pick up their responsibilities in life. They may be aggressively exploitive, like those who physically abuse others, or they may be more subtle, like the manipulative con artist. Controllers use force, shrewd argument and guilt to accomplish their ends. It is difficult for them to recognize their boundary problems. Controllers feel so right about the priority of getting their needs and desires met that they believe they are justified in using any means to get what they want.

The problem with Controllers is that they are not really *in control,* but are *controlled* by their own appetites and desires. This is the spoiled child who always bullied his parents or threw temper tantrums until his parents caved in and gave him what he wanted. Eventually, nothing satisfied him. Lurking beneath the surface of the Controller's psyche is the fear that if he stops controlling and manipulating, he will be abandoned. Missing from the Controller's life is the experience he needs most—to be loved and cared for as a person, to receive love that has not been coerced.

Nonresponsives do not hear the needs of others. A typical scenario might play out this way: A wife expresses her feelings of hurt to her husband, who responds by saying, "Grow up! Life's tough. I've got my own stuff to worry about." This husband has not truly listened to the crying need of his wife.

Philippians 2:4 says, "Each of you should look not only to your own interests, but also to the interests of others." This verse is particularly important for our understanding of boundaries. It affirms a biblically appropriate concern for our own needs while balancing this concern with a loving regard for the needs of others. God wants us to take care of ourselves so that we will be in a position to meet the needs of others.

Nonresponsives have often been deeply hurt by others in the past. Sometimes they are recovering Compliants who become so sensitive to their former pattern of always saying yes that they say no to everything out of fear of falling into their old habits. Compliants often feel used and violated. So it's understandable when their walls of defense become so thick that they are unresponsive to the needs of others. It's understandable, but not healthy. The walls keep everything out—the good as well as the bad.

Love requires an appropriate willingness to say yes. Nonresponsives who have been hurt, such as the recovering Compliant, can learn to trust and love others again.

Avoidants say no to the good. Some men and women cannot ask for help when they need it and cannot seem to accept love when it's offered. For some reason Avoidants see having needs or problems as bad. If we grew up in an atmosphere where we were only praised when we did things well, we may be unwilling to acknowledge our problems or weaknesses for fear of being ridiculed or losing another person's respect or love. If we suffer from low self-esteem, then it will be difficult for us to admit to others our need for help or support.

Men have an especially difficult time accepting help or advice. Many men today live in a world of competition, where admitting to weakness or expressing a need will be used against them. Yet men in the Christian community are beginning to show that they are serious about learning to listen better and bear one another's burdens, without taking advantage of another's weakness or abusing a confidence. God wants us to mutually support and care for one another. Learning to admit our needs openly and let others love us may be one of the most difficult boundary problems we face.

It is easy to see how the various boundary problems feed on one another. An ugly relational mix occurs when a weak Compliant meets an aggressive Controller. There will be abuse in this relationship. And we can also have composite boundary problems. A person might be a Compliant/Avoidant. We have all known people who insist on doing everything for everyone else, but will not allow anyone to do anything for them.

Husbands and wives will benefit from healthy discussions about where we struggle with boundary problems and how we might address the issues involved. We can practice putting off falsehood and speaking the truth to one another in love. If you continually struggle as a couple to break unhealthy patterns, see a marriage and family counselor. Often it is difficult for us to break through a lifetime of knee-jerk responses without the help of a skillful and perceptive third person. Learning more about our boundaries can be the key to better communication, greater mutual respect, and experiencing deeper and more loving relationships in our families.

Boundary Issues in Parenting

At the core of healthy personality is the unshakable assurance that one is loved. In chapter three we noted that this emotionally centered feeling of safety and significance begins as we experience a successful bond with our mothers. The strong mother bond creates for the child a base of trust and courage. The internalized presence of a good and loving mother is the platform from which a child will relate with others throughout life.

God is the author of the mother bond. He knew that in order for us to love others, we needed to experience an unfailing love that does not depend on our achievements or abilities. A mother's constant presence is our first human experience of this kind of love. As we mature we learn about an even greater and more abiding love, the love God has for us. But our understanding of real love begins with a caring mother who is there for us in the earliest stages of our lives.

Chapter two highlighted the important role fathers play in the various stages of separation that children undergo on their journey toward maturity. Children mature as they achieve independence from their mothers. The father acts as a second significant love object for the child that assists in this individuation process. These early life stages are the incubation period for the formation of healthy boundaries.

We want our children to grow up as adults who do not exhibit the characteristics of Compliants, Controllers, Nonresponsives or Avoidants. Teaching our children healthy boundaries, and ensuring that all family members respect those boundaries, gives children the secure space they need to learn how to love. Here are some key ideas to keep in mind as we take on this essential task.

First, parents need to work on creating a home environment in which boundaries are consistently taught and lived out in a loving manner. Inconsistency leads to insecurity in children and a variety of boundary problems in later life. I recently taught a class in which a young woman, Sharon, explained to others what it was like to grow up in a home with an alcoholic mother. Her mom would be loving and gentle in the morning and explosive and abusive when Sharon came home from school. The next day would be the complete opposite. Sharon never felt safe. She tried desperately to please her mother, working harder and harder to win her love.

Sharon is still living out these destructive patterns even though she has been married and living on her own for years. She is unable to maintain healthy boundaries in her professional life. A low self-esteem drives her to excessive workaholism as she constantly tries to gain affirmation through her performance. She is perfectionistic; no accomplishment is ever good enough. Sharon is as hard on herself now as her mother was hard on her when she was growing up. She has problems in her marriage because she can't say no at work. Her husband, Steve, tells her he feels like he is the only one she ever says no to. They never have enough time together.

Second, no matter how difficult our children become for us, it is absolutely necessary to stay connected with them emotionally when we are going through a tough time. Our kids need to know that our love for them is not dependent on their behavior. Staying emotionally present as you discipline does not give the message that you are consenting to your child's bad behavior. Our children need to experience the consequences of their choices. We will have time-outs, will even spank when it's appropriate, but we will not withhold our love. Sometimes the most loving thing we do is to let our children see our honest anger.

A child needs to learn that a parent can be angry yet maintain control while expressing love. It is helpful to tell your child why you are angry and when you will deal with the conflict. Then work out appropriate discipline and any change that needs to occur to keep the situation from happening again. It is not helpful to blow up and leave for an extended period of time, or to punish your child with long periods of the silent treatment. In cases like these the child's behavior has led to an experience of abandonment and isolation. This is especially confusing for the child when a parent who has left comes back hours later and acts as if nothing ever happened. There is never any satisfactory resolution to the conflict that occurred.

On the other hand, if a child experiences a parent's anger but the parent stays and works through the situation to a point of resolution, the child learns about honest, confrontational love. The child's disobedience does not lead to abandonment but resolution of conflict through the parent's continued involvement. And the love shown in good conflict resolution results in an even better relationship for both child and parent in the future.

Even spanking can be administered in such a way that Dad or Mom remains lovingly connected with the child through the experience. (I'm talking here about a spanking, not a beating, and only when the children are younger.) I remember the times right after spanking one of our children as some of the closest moments I have shared with our kids. When one of them crossed that final frontier and a spanking had to be administered, it had the effect of getting us quickly past the problem and restoring right relationship again. Forgiveness was granted immediately. We always hugged and held our kids after spanking. It was a good time to talk. They knew that whatever they had done did not change the way we felt about them. Nothing they could ever do would make us love them less.

Third, we need to realize that "no" coming from the mouths of our children can be just as loving a response as "yes." We want our kids to be free to say things like "No, that's wrong!" "That's bad!" "I don't want to do that!" "Stop, that hurts!" Children need to learn to say no to things that are wrong or bad.

Our son Gabe was a strong-willed child. His first word was "no"! And he said it whenever someone spoke to him, just to make sure right up front that he was not going to do something, or go somewhere, or eat anything he didn't want to. Judie and I were tough on Gabe when he was younger. He was always in trouble because of his iron will. What we did not understand very well then, but we see more clearly now, is that a certain amount of willfulness has to be carefully maintained and encouraged in your child or other problems will surface.

Judie and I both possess strong personalities. We took Gabe on and won; Gabe became compliant. This made him wonderful to be around during the elementary years, and he is still a beautiful and pleasant person. But his struggles during the teenage years have been with peer pressure and an inability to say no to things that are wrong and bad for him. We had taught Gabe that his "no" was wrong and would lead to punishment. It is only recently that Judie and I have seen how important it is to let Gabe really be himself and honestly disagree with us. Things are not as easy that way, but they are a whole lot healthier. It is never too late to realize our mistakes and work to correct them.

Another kind of no we need to hear and respect from our kids is the no related to their needs for privacy. We have to be very sensitive to when it is no longer appropriate for Mom or Dad to help with the bath, or when our kids begin to feel the need for privacy while dressing. We need to let our children say no to our help, to allow them freedom to do things themselves, even if they fail (or look a little sloppy after dressing themselves for church). This is the way they learn who they are in relation to the world around them. If we are overly protective of our children, they cannot establish a strong sense of their own boundaries in relationship with others. They need to find out who they are by pushing against the boundaries of the outside world.

Another no we need to hear—one that may be tough for us—is when our children begin to resist our parental shows of affection. Our children need the freedom to explore what is right for them in these sensitive emotional areas. Your daughter will probably go through a phase like our daughter, Jana, did. She came to a point in her physical development when she felt uncomfortable hugging Dad with a full body hug. Reticence to hug or kiss Mom and Dad in public is another "no" we need to respect when the time comes. These are natural transitions our kids go through that help them establish healthy boundaries. We need to allow them room to discover their own comfort zones in these areas.

Daughters will most often mature to become women who find it easy and natural to hug their dads. And little boys will grow into men who feel very comfortable kissing their mothers again, even in public. But they need the freedom to work these things out. As parents, we have an obligation to respect them as they explore their boundaries.

Children will also need to learn how to accept the no of others. They cannot be allowed to dominate their world with aggressive and controlling behaviors. Temper tantrums should not be tolerated. Proverbs 19:18 says, "Discipline your son, for in that there is hope; do not be a willing party to his death." Hearing a no from others is an important part of life. It is the way our children learn to respect the boundaries of others. They should be able to hear "no" without feeling put down, rejected or hurt. Our children should increasingly realize that life will present many conflicts in relationship that need to be resolved through dialogue in a context of love and mutual respect. This is what Paul calls "speaking the truth in love" (Eph 4:15).

Developing healthy boundaries in our children is a real balancing act for us as parents. We need to discipline our children well, so that they learn self-control through experiencing the uncomfortable consequences that naturally flow from making bad choices. But if we control our children too much or are overly protective, they become dependent and struggle to set boundaries for themselves. These children are afraid to take risks. They play it safe. And if they do try to break away from parental control, it usually comes in the form of strong rebellion during the teenage years.

We need to let our children learn to say appropriate no's. But if we do not moderate this, our children will grow up thinking the world owes them and is theirs for the asking. A little boy who continually gets what he wants by throwing a temper tantrum will grow up to be a man who tries to control his environment through aggressive, domineering behavior. He will not be able to hear no from others. And the worst part about this is that he has never developed a sensitivity to the needs of others; he is a selfish person who has no compassion. He does not really know how to love.

Knowing what it takes to develop good boundaries in our children does not necessarily make parenting easier. But at least it helps us to know what we're aiming for in this complex dimension of contemporary family life.

Abusing the Boundaries: Emotional Incest

The flip side of staying emotionally present with your children is the boundary problem of being too emotionally involved, or enmeshed, with them. This problem is often referred to as *emotional incest*. Some parents turn to their children rather than their spouses or friends for emotional support. From the outside this parent may appear to others as extremely loving and caring. The parent spends a great deal of time with the son or daughter. But in reality this love is not a nurturing, other-directed love but a controlling ploy of the parent to satisfy selfish, unmet needs at the child's expense.

I remember working with a distressed mom, Wanda, who described this kind of relationship between her husband and their daughter. She had kept her feelings buried for years, thinking she was just jealous of the good relationship Bill had with Heidi. But later, when Wanda started to realize that Heidi had no peer friends in later elementary school and junior high, and that her father was her only friend, Wanda began to wonder about the health of the relationship. Bill was even planning regular ski trips to Tahoe that included his daughter but excluded his wife.

When Wanda tried to bring up the fact that she was bothered by the situation, Bill and Heidi teamed up against her and told her she was crazy. They would laugh at her and talk about her behind her back. This hurt Wanda even more. But behind the anger and pain there was honest concern for Bill and Heidi. And Wanda worried about her marriage. She could see how difficult life was going to be for Heidi when she went off to college. She said Heidi had never been given permission by her father to enter into her own world of friends, to get a job or even to study without her father's help. (Bill was an engineer, and Heidi, who excelled in math, wanted to be an engineer like her dad.) Heidi always felt very special because of her father's doting on her—the trips, the gifts, meals out together to talk privately as friends. But what was going to happen when the real world caught up to her?

Wanda's concerns for Heidi were justifiable. Children who grow up playing the role of primary emotional support for one of their parents will often face a variety of problems later. Children are unprepared for the complexities of adult relationships. When children are exposed to a father's secret confessions and hidden irritations with his wife, they are robbed of a normal childhood. And they will suffer for it later. They often experience pervasive guilt when they choose to develop a life of their own. They are confused about why they feel this way, finding it hard to blame a parent who has done so much for them, spent so much time with them and confided in them so deeply. A child who has been the victim of emotional incest will often suffer many of the boundary problems of a child who has been molested or sexually abused.

This kind of enmeshment is always difficult to identify as a problem because the early behaviors look so much like love and good parenting. But a loving mother can be too loving. She can smother her kids and not allow them the freedom to develop into the mature, independent individuals God intends them to be. Such mothers need their children more than the children need them. Fathers and mothers who make their young children their best friends are usually taking advantage of the vulnerability and weakness of their children. They are satisfying their needs at the expense of the normal needs of their son or daughter. These individuals have usually not been able to achieve healthy adult relationships. And instead of getting help to work through their problems, they fill their emptiness by establishing an unhealthy relationship with a child who is easy to control and manipulate.

There are two resources I would recommend if you need to know more about this boundary problem: Patricia Love's *The Emotional Incest Syndrome: What to Do When a Parent's Love Rules Your Life* and Laurie Ashner and Mitch Meyerson's *When Parents Love Too Much*. These two books have been very helpful to a number of people.

The Boundary Abuse of Incest and Molestation

Ed's face was white with pain and anger. He said, "I have wanted to kill the guy who molested my daughter. . . . But I didn't kill him because the guy who molested my daughter was me."[2]

What a child is supposed to learn from a parent is how to have a healthy relationship with others. This is what boundaries are all about. We discover where we leave off and the rest of the world begins. We distinguish between what belongs to others and what belongs to us. Parents who sexually invade their child's boundaries inflict enormous pain and suffering.

A child who has been sexually abused will conclude that having sex is a necessary part of what it means to be in relationship (if

[137]

these abusive experiences are not repressed). These children grow up vulnerable to sexual invasion, especially by those in positions of power—pastors, psychologists, doctors, bosses, controllers. Abused children also grow up with a trained predisposition to molest and invade others. This is why it is so common for abuse to span many generations in a particular family. Most of those who experience sexual abuse find it extremely difficult to relearn the values of healthy sexuality. They are unable to freely enjoy— with someone who loves them—an experience that for years has brought them confusion, pain and feelings of deep shame.

The number of children molested every day is steadily rising. Conservative estimates are that one out of every five girls and one out of every eight boys is a victim of sexual abuse before reaching age twelve.[3]

An elder in our church told me recently that he was called for jury duty on a sexual molestation case. There were twenty prospective jurors in the room, eleven women and nine men. The judge told the jurors that anyone who had experienced sexual abuse or molestation would be excused. Seven of the women immediately responded that they would be unfit to serve. Two others asked if they could talk with the judge privately. They were both excused. Bob was astonished to discover that from a random sample of computer-generated names, nine out of eleven women had probably been molested or sexually abused.

We know that in the largest number of these cases the offender is someone in the child's own family. Seventy-seven percent of the offenders are the victim's parents. Of this group of parental offenders, 79 percent are fathers and 21 percent are mothers. Sixteen percent of nonparental abusers are other relatives.[4]

Incest is always an act of violence. Here there is a true victim, a powerless child, overpowered by a powerful parent. The parent's lust is like a toxic flood that washes away all of the boundaries of a child's life, leaving in its path physical, mental, emotional and spiritual devastation. The person sitting in the seat of power holds

[138]

all the cards. The child victim is pressured into secrecy about the sexual activity or made to feel guilty and at fault. Often the child's body physically responds to the sexual stimulation, making the child feel even more guilty and confused. Normally the child believes that he or she has nowhere to turn for help and no acceptable way out.

A friend of mine shared with me that she repeatedly told her mother about the sexual abuse of her father. Her mother responded by telling her it was all in her imagination—her father loved her and would never do anything to hurt her.

If you are a mother, it is especially important that you not live in denial concerning sexual abuse. Be wise if you suspect that anything out of the ordinary may be occurring in your family. Denial is powerful here because if you admit the possibility that your husband may be abusing your daughter(s) or your son(s), you have suddenly stepped into a relational mine field that has the potential to blow your family apart. But the situation must be faced with strength, courage and wisdom.

Your child has to be your primary consideration. If you respond with disbelief, uncontrollable anger or accusations against your child, you will close off communication that at this critical and fragile moment needs to be encouraged. You are only revictimizing the victim, your helpless child. If you become angry, make sure your son or daughter understands that you are not angry at him or her, but at the one who did this.

An abused son needs to feel that you are willing to believe him and act on his behalf. An abused daughter needs to feel safe with you. She needs to know that you realize this is not her fault, and that you love her. A son or daughter sharing a problem with you needs to be assured that you are there to help and will make certain the abuse never occurs again. Researchers agree that the most important element in a child's recovery from the pain of molestation or incest is *the parent's support and belief that what the child is reporting is true.*[5]

Family situations of incest and molestation are very complex. Don't try to handle this privately. Seek professional help from someone you trust. You are dealing with not only a multitude of difficult issues related to your son or daughter but also issues in your marriage and with your husband, wife, or other family member. You will also need help to keep from putting unnecessary guilt and blame on yourself as you work through this time that has shocked you and sent your world spinning. You need someone to help you know that the feelings you are experiencing are normal for what you are going through. You need someone who can say to you with conviction, "You and your daughter can heal and recover. There is hope for your family. With God in your lives, this abuse is not the end of the story."

The victims of sexual abuse need help in gaining emotional strength and wholeness. The family needs to understand and overcome any unhealthy patterns of relating that may have allowed the abuse to go on. The violator needs to be held accountable for his or her actions. Any potential restoration of the family must begin with the violator accepting full responsibility for the abuse.

If a father sins in this way, his only recourse is to openly admit his selfishness to the entire family, to seek help for himself and his wounded wife and children, and to beg forgiveness from his daughter and from God. He will have to sincerely express to all that he realizes this sin is his and his alone. He is responsible.

A mother who has abused her child needs to come to the same place of accepting full responsibility for what happened and confessing her sin to the abused son or daughter and to her spouse. From this foundation of truth and confession the restoration process can begin. Only when all attempts to justify or minimize what occurred are put aside can full and meaningful forgiveness take place and healthy relationships be restored.

There is always hope. I read the account of a young woman named Kathleen. She tells of her father's incestuous relationship with her. Kathleen ends her story this way:

I think now of my past as though it is a scrapbook and not a newspaper. Newspapers are filled with current events containing a little history or perspective. But a scrapbook is filled with significant memories and stories.

An incest survivor who never enters into the pain of her past carries yesterday inside of her. She is bound to her pain. As I've worked through the images of my childhood, I've been able to let them go and in a real sense put those pictures into a special place, an honored place in my life. . . . Filled with important pictures of yesterday, my scrapbook is there when I need to look at it. I can look through the pictures, and I can put it back on the shelf. I am not chained to my past.

I do not expect my life to be perfect. Sin has fractured all of our lives. . . . But "he who began a good work in you will carry it on to completion" (Phil 1:6). God's grace is the "stuff" of my healing. The journey goes on; the healing not only of years past but of yesterday deepens; and I am filled with hope.

On my bedroom wall hangs a verse (Jer 29:11) which I've cross-stitched as a reminder: "For I know the plans I have for you . . . to give you hope and a future."[6]

The Boundaries of God

Is there a strong biblical basis for the principles discussed here? The answer to that is a resounding yes. All of what is significant about love and relational boundaries is rooted in the character and behavior of God.

God speaks the truth to us in love, defining his personality in relation to us with language that reveals his plans and purposes for our life together in the family. He tells us who he is and who he is not, his likes and dislikes. He makes clear what he will and will not allow to go on in his yard, what he is responsible for and what we are responsible for—all with the goal of maintaining true and honest relationships. If we understand biblical love, we will understand what it means to have and live with healthy boundaries in place.

1. Biblical love refuses to violate another's boundaries. Biblical love is not characterized by sentimental feelings, but by a determination to act responsibly in relation to God and others. This is what boundaries are all about. God's commandments essentially define what it means to act respectfully toward the boundaries of others.

Paul writes, "Let no debt remain outstanding, except the continuing debt to love one another, for he who loves his fellow man has fulfilled the law. The commandments, 'Do not commit adultery,' 'Do not murder,' 'Do not steal,' 'Do not covet,' and whatever other commandment there may be, are summed up in this one rule: 'Love your neighbor as yourself.' Love does no harm to its neighbor. Therefore love is the fulfillment of the law" (Rom 13:8-10).

Adultery, for instance, is a chosen behavior that shows our disrespect for and violation of a covenant relationship. We have made a promise that creates a boundary. Our promises made to one another erect a protective fence around our marriage relationship. If the husband or wife climbs over that fence, physical and emotional boundaries are violated and trust is broken. A covenant commitment is a boundary that has to be honored and kept.

We can murder someone by taking his life. We can also murder by violating another's soul. This is the essence of sin, killing what is uniquely valuable in another to satisfy some selfish desire. James says, "What causes fights and quarrels among you? Don't they come from your desires that battle within you? You want something but don't get it. You kill and covet, but you cannot have what you want" (Jas 4:1-2). We murder when our lusts spill over and poison relationships, diminishing another person for our pleasure or selfish desires.

Coveting is an envious attitude that creates separation between ourselves and others. It can even lead to the physical act of stealing from others that to which we have no right. Coveting shows no respect for the boundaries of others. Our selfishness washes away proper boundaries, destroying a healthy acceptance of who we are and imprisoning us in unhealthy comparisons that violate the boundaries of others and damage relationships. "Each one should test his own actions," Paul writes. "Then he can take pride in himself, without comparing himself to somebody else, for each one should carry his own load" (Gal 6:4-5).

Love means taking responsibility for our lives in relationship to God. And love refuses to violate the boundaries, as God clearly defines them, for living in loving relationship with others. Paul says the law can be summarized in this way: " 'Love your neighbor as yourself.' Love does no harm to its neighbor. Therefore love is the fulfillment of the law" (Rom 13:9-10). This is powerful boundary language.

2. Biblical love speaks truthfully. "Therefore each of you must put off falsehood and speak truthfully to his neighbor, for we are all members of one body" (Eph 4:25). This verse says two things. First, we are to speak truthfully. Love requires honestly confronting others with our true feelings in a spirit of grace. This is the way we grow to a mature understanding of important relational boundaries in our families. Good relationships require this kind of honesty. Pain is good if it leads to healing and deeper understanding. If we try to bury our anger and hurt, bitterness sets in. This is what kills trust in our family relationships.

The other half of the Ephesians verse emphasizes that we are to "put off falsehood." In the language of boundaries this strongly suggests that we need a willingness to share openly who we are rather than keep our boundaries hidden. It is a loving thing to be bold enough to let others know what we like or dislike, what is comfortable or painful for us, what our expectations are in regard to our relationship, how much we can give without feeling taken advantage of and how we would like to receive the love that others offer.

Putting off falsehood is a risk we have to learn to take if we are ever really going to live freely and interact joyfully with those who are in our lives. If we don't make our boundaries known, the trespassing of our hidden boundaries will continually stir up unnecessary inner resentment and anger in us.

3. Biblical love overcomes our fears. The Bible says, "There is no fear in love. But perfect love drives out fear, because fear has to do with punishment. The one who fears is not made perfect in love" (1 Jn 4:18). Our fears often stand between us and others. This is especially true if our boundaries have been violated in the past. We are afraid of being rejected, of being on the receiving end of another's anger, of having our hidden secrets discovered, of being alone.

The family is a wonderful place to risk tearing down some of these walls, to learn to let others love us. As we share who we really are with others in the family and our real person is accepted and affirmed, we build the family fabric of trust. As our trust grows, the depth and quality of our family relationships grow. God can help us all to set aside our fears and risk letting others know who we really are. God can help us as parents to love our children so thoroughly that they will trust us enough to fearlessly let us know who they really are.

4. Biblical love is not motivated by guilt. God motivates us to grow and change and act on the basis of love, not guilt. We are moved by God's unconditional love, that he would love us so much that he would allow his only Son to die for us, to free us from the bondage of sin. It is interesting that the Bible really does not deal with the concept of guilty feelings. A word study on *guilt* in the Bible reveals that the word is reserved for our state of being prior to accepting Christ. The Bible does not affirm using guilt as a strategy and motivating force to bring about life change in others. We should not lay guilt trips on others, and we need to learn to recognize and resist when we are being manipulated by guilt.

In their book on boundaries, Henry Cloud and John Townsend describe how guilt messages work on us if we have weak boundaries. A weak person will likely internalize guilt messages and respond to manipulation without thinking. Many guilt messages come disguised in God-talk, like when you tell your mother that you can't make it home for Thanksgiving and she says, "Doesn't the Bible teach that you're supposed to honor your parents?" Or when you lovingly confront a "friend" and hear him say, "How can you call yourself a Christian and treat me like this?" These are powerful statements that can eat away at the heart of a person who is unsure of his or her boundaries.

Here is how Cloud and Townsend suggest we handle manipulative messages that are attempts to control us through guilt.[7]

Recognize guilt messages. If we are vulnerable to this kind of manipulation, we will often respond without recognizing that we are being controlled. We need to learn to sniff out the guilt message and take control of the situation rather than being controlled by it. The message aimed at controlling us through guilt is not motivated by love or care for us. It is emotional blackmail.

Guilt messages are really anger, sadness or hurt in disguise. Those who send you a guilt message are usually covering up feelings of anger or hurt. They cannot honestly express their true feelings, so they shift the responsibility onto you. We need to recognize these shifts and learn to point them out to others when the guilt message surfaces. "It sounds like you're angry with me because I don't have time to come over today. I'm sorry you feel that way. I'll call you tomorrow and we can talk about it." Cloud and Townsend write, "Empathize with the distress people are feeling, but make it clear that it is *their* distress."[8]

If guilt works on you, recognize that this is your problem and not the other person's. If we respond to guilt messages, we do not have adequate and healthy boundaries. Don't blame others for laying a guilt trip on you. Take responsibility for your life by refusing to be manipulated. This will save you a lot of trouble and a lot of inner bitterness and anger. Recognize that as long as others can *make* you feel guilty, and you only feel good when they stop *making* you feel this way, *they* are in control of your life.

Do not feel compelled to explain or justify your behavior. You do not owe an explanation to someone who is trying to manipulate you through guilt. Simply express your intentions and choice and move on. Your deep desire to have others fully understand and absolve your choices shows that you are still under their control. You are not free to make your own choices based on the appropriate and healthy boundaries in your life. If others have the power to make you react, they are inside your territory. They are creating the rules that govern your life choices.

We need to make sure that others know that we hear their pain or hurt or need and empathize with them. We always want to think clearly about the nature of our true responsibility to others as a loving person. But we cannot let others control our lives through guilt. Neither person is served in a relationship governed by manipulation. The goal of authentic relationships is honest communication and a genuine demonstration of love and respect that honors the freedom of both individuals to keep their boundaries intact.

5. Biblical love maintains a place for honest anger. God himself gets angry and expresses his anger (Ex 4:14; Deut 29:27). God openly expresses his anger when we violate his boundaries through sin and disobedience. Anger can often be a healthy emotion that arises when someone tries to manipulate or control us. Anger should operate as an early warning signal that something in a relationship needs to be dealt with openly and honestly. Anger is really our friend. It leads us into deeper honesty, helps us to keep shorter accounts and warns us that we need to act to make something right.[9]

These biblical guidelines give us a picture of what it means to love ourselves and others in a godly manner. Healthy, biblically based boundaries help us all to live from Christ-centered strength in our families, confidently saying no to what is bad or wrong and yes to what is good and right.

Questions for Discussion

1. If you had to identify an area where you would characteristically struggle with boundary issues, would you say your struggle is more as a Compliant, a Controller, a Nonresponsive or an Avoidant?

2. What suggestions from the section on helping children with boundaries did you find particularly meaningful? How will you apply the ideas to your home situation?

3. Discuss how a parent can stay lovingly connected with a child even while the parent is experiencing anger or acting decisively to discipline.

4. Discuss together why it is important to allow our children to say appropriate no's. Why is teaching and training a child in this area such a difficult balancing act?

5. The author says, "If guilt works on you, recognize that this is your problem and not the other person's." Do you agree? What can you do to gain conrol of your life if responding to guilt messages has been your pattern in the past?

10
Tempted to Be a Couch Potato Family

•

The nameless woman in her welfare flat does not look directly into the television camera, but stares blankly at the floor beneath her feet. The lights bother her eyes. She is in her early twenties. She looks much older, forty or more, way too thin, black skin blanched whitish and too tight over a bony face and bare arms, hands trembling. The interviewer asks her why she does drugs. She is slow to answer.

In the background the ceiling is crumbling where the roof leaks, and pieces of it lie in a pile in the corner. The walls are streaked with dirt. Cigarette burns mark the top of the card table, the arm of the sofa, the small brown square of thin carpet covering a concrete floor. Red, blue, green and yellow plastic dishes are stacked to overflowing in the sink and scattered aimlessly along the counter.

"It makes me feel good, I guess," she mumbles. Then after a few seconds, "I get bored with this." She nods in the direction of the mess behind her.

The TV camera pans the two-room flat. "Where do you get money for the drugs?" you hear the interviewer ask.

The woman's two kids—three and five years old—ignore the

whole scene. They sit slumped on the concrete in front of the television set, staring.

"I dress and go out," she says, looking up to see what the man thinks. "I turn a trick or two when I need it," she whispers.

The kids giggle out loud behind her at something on the tube. The older toddler shifts the position of his legs slightly, then settles down to watch some more.

Shooting Tube

A brief article by Pete Hamill first alerted me to the intriguing similarities between taking drugs and watching TV. He was exploring the drug problem in the United States and asking the question "Why do so many millions of Americans of all ages, races, and classes choose to spend all or part of their lives stupefied?"[1]

Hamill interviewed drug addicts who talked about escaping the pain and boredom of life. Drugs served as a convenient and accessible alternative to emptiness and despair. There have always been drug addicts. But in earlier generations in North America experimentation with drugs was the experience of relatively few, usually those living in small, counterculture pockets of society. Today Western nations are drowning in drugs—to the tune of $120 billion a year in the United States. The transition from a marginal drug culture in American life to a dominant one coincides with the advent of television. Two generations of young people have now grown up under its influence.

On the surface it may sound like quite a stretch to connect watching television with drug addiction. But there are some startling similarities between the two experiences. Television absorbs its viewers in the same ways that drugs consume their users. It works on the same imaginative and intellectual level as psychoactive drugs. While shooting tube, viewers normally cannot work, play, read, reason or use their creative imaginations. They are also unable to relate to others while turned on to TV. Shooting tube

[149]

provides a high—a momentary escape from the boredom and pain of everyday existence.[2]

Perhaps television's most devastating effect is the way it predisposes young minds to look for an entertaining escape when real life becomes painful or boring. Young people are being trained in addictive behavior before they're even old enough to know what drugs are. Drugs and alcohol are a natural next step when kids grow older and discover that these things are as readily available in their schools and neighborhoods as TVs are in their homes. It's not just ghetto kids and families that are affected here. This is the state of our society today.

Television Addicts

The first thing that is wrong with TV, then, is that it becomes an addictive pastime for millions upon millions of men, women and children. It simply gobbles up thousands of hours that could be put to better use in our personal lives, our families, our churches and neighborhoods.

Children today watch twice as much television as their parents did. On the average, they spend more time in front of the TV than they do attending class. A third of all school-age children are still watching television at eleven o'clock at night. A major impact of shooting this much tube is that time spent on homework has taken a nosedive. Students in the mid-seventies averaged ten hours of homework a week. By the late eighties, that figure had dropped to five hours a week. Twenty percent of high-school teens now do no homework. Most analysts blame these poor study habits on the failure of families to monitor their TV viewing.[3]

How addicted are our kids? One Michigan State University study in the early eighties offered a group of four- and five-year-olds the choice of giving up TV or giving up their fathers. A third of the children said they would give up their daddies. Pete Hamill notes that given a similar choice between giving up cocaine or a father, mother, brother, sister, wife, husband, children or job, al-

[150]

most any junkie would do the same.[4]

How addicted are we? A recent *TV Guide* poll tried to find out how much money it would take for American viewers to give up watching TV for life. They found that 46 percent of all American TV viewers would not give up their televisions for less than one million dollars. Twenty-five percent said they wouldn't give up watching TV even for a million dollars. Of Americans who made less than twenty thousand dollars a year, the same percentage, a fourth of those polled, would not give up watching TV even for a million dollars—the equivalent of fifty years' salary.[5]

How many hours of TV does your family watch in a typical week? Any amount of time given to watching television generally diverts us from doing other worthwhile things. Watching an enriching television program can be an excellent experience for us and for our families. But most of our television viewing is purely an entertaining way of passing time. Even if we are watching with our families, we seldom interact with them during or even after a program. TV isolates us from others, even if they are in the same room. And many families have TVs scattered throughout the house. Seventy-five percent of American families own more than one TV, and 15 percent have three or more.[6] Family members can shoot tube in the seclusion of their own rooms, which only adds to our isolation from one another.

An evening is a terrible thing to waste. A life is a terrible thing to waste. Television is perhaps the greatest time consumer in the average family's life. Families desperately need more time to interact with each other, even if it is simply an afternoon or evening of playing games. Family time is precious for us today. What kids remember most about their childhoods is the times they spent together as a family, talking, laughing and enjoying each other. As families we need more time to work together, plan together, read together, create together and solve real problems together. But so much of this time can simply vanish if we are a family of couch potatoes, addicted to the tube.

Some families want to interact more effectively but don't know where to start because they have had so little practice at it. We spend less and less time with each other. We are separated by work and school during the day and by private TV watching in the evening. We start this isolation process by using the TV as a baby-sitter when our kids are very young. Pretty soon kids become bored with family activities because Mom and Dad simply can't compete with a million-dollar thirty-second commercial filled with action-packed, riveting special effects.

Will the Real *Prime Time* Please Stand Up?

All of this TV watching creates confusion in our minds and in the minds of our kids about real life. Our minds suck up hours upon hours of prime-time TV images—images of life that for the most part create false expectations about how life should operate. Then we are ill-equipped to actually think, relate and work in the prime-time world as it really is. Regular consumption of the unrealistic worldviews offered by TV runs contrary to our attempts to teach and model godly truth.

If we think about it, we know that everything that's worth anything in life is acquired through human energy and commitment. Somehow we have to encourage in our kids a growing love for accomplishment through effort. It takes effort, for instance, to read and think. Reading forces us to connect ideas, to create images in our minds, to interact with an author like we would dialogue with an intelligent friend. It is an experience that challenges us to use our imaginations. When is the last time you saw anyone on TV reading a book?

Children should be read to frequently and should have an abundance of time to read on their own. Parents need to discuss with their kids the meaning of stories and nonfiction materials the children read. Children should get a lot of encouragement to use their minds creatively by making up stories and drawing pictures. They need more creative time with a lot of encouragement and affirmation and less TV time. Otherwise they will fall into thinking that their creative work isn't worth anything because it cannot compete with the powerful images they see created on TV.

Television, by the very nature of the medium, lures its viewers into passivity. It discourages rational analysis. Television moves too fast to allow for much imaginative interaction. Before you have time to stop and consider the meaning or significance of something that has just happened, you are drawn into the next scene, which overrides the preceding moment. Viewers are necessarily passive. They move along at the pace of the program they are watching, laughing with the laugh tracks and experiencing unearned emotions hyped by technique and technology. Quentin Schultze compares the way we watch TV to the way a cow watches passing cars. "The eyes are open, and some type of sensation is generated in the brain of the bovine. But there is no critical mental activity, no power of interpretation or evaluation."[7]

It takes clear thinking and patient determination to solve the difficult problems of life. But prime-time dramas and sitcoms give us the overall impression that life is easy. Every day major family crises are solved in half an hour with three commercial breaks. This kind of oversimplification occurs even in high-quality entertainment programs. In one of my favorite TV dramas, police detectives take half an hour to investigate complex crimes, including tracking down, interrogating and arresting the criminals. Then the district attorney's office takes over. They are able to research, build and try their case to completion, all in less than an hour.

We see this happen with such regularity on TV that we begin to think this is the way life should go for us. When it doesn't, the temptation is to check out or shoot some more tube. It makes us feel good. We do not learn how to manage life well by watching TV. And the biblical truth, wisdom and values we need for deciding the major issues in life are conspicuously absent from prime-time programming.

[153]

It also takes effort and commitment to sustain worthwhile real-life relationships. We need to learn how to live together and love one another, what it takes to be a real friend, a real father or mother, a real lover and a real person creatively engaged in real life. TV love relationships are too easy. If you wear the right clothes and cologne, you get the girl—it's that simple. Love in real life is not that simple. Real love requires responsible and sustained commitment over the long haul; it's about facing the many painful struggles of life together and learning how to persevere, steadily growing in love. Television does not prepare us for this. Love on TV has nothing to do with responsibility. People fall in love, jump into bed (they always have great sex the first time they're together, wherever that might be) and stay together as long as the romantic bliss remains. When the bloom withers, the man and woman break it off and go their separate ways—in search of another love episode, with no apparent sense that anything significant has been gained or lost.

TV also presents a highly glamorized work life. The tube is monopolized by doctors, lawyers, writers, models, entertainers and cops (even police work is idealized and romanticized). The lifestyles of the rich and famous captivate viewers. This too can create unrealistic expectations that make it hard to live in the real world of work. Ideas like starting at the bottom and working your way up and the importance of hard work and dedication are not popular themes on television today.

Prime-time themes like "You can get rich quick" and "Wealth is the root of all happiness" captivate us. Yet few young people today are able to graduate from college and get a solid position in the field of their choice. Most wind up taking whatever they can get. But if they don't get immediate promotions, they jump to something else. There is tremendous frustration in young people today regarding work options or the lack of them. Television does not prepare us for this reality. When the majority of programs on television picture a vocational world so completely different from what occurs in the real prime-time world of work, the false expectations created become harmful, even dangerous.

If present trends continue, more and more young people will just "drop out," like they did in the mid-sixties. Drugs will continue to be a major problem for our youth because they have been trained by shooting tube to check out when life becomes difficult. Young people will be increasingly frustrated by the difference between their expectations of what life should be like as depicted on television and what it takes to live life as it really is. They will find it difficult to confront the harsh realities of life without a pause button or the ability to quickly switch to something better or more exciting by remote control.

We will not be able to teach our children self-discipline and the benefits of hard work if television and its message have more time with our children than we do. We will not be able to teach our children how to think and use their creative imaginations if the passive act of watching TV is the dominant mental activity (or inactivity) of their lives. We will not be able to teach our children how to relate effectively with others within and outside the family if their available relational time is spent isolated from others in the fastest-growing American pastime, TV hibernation. We will certainly not be able to encourage our kids to read, enjoy and create art, study God's Word, think, relate to others, work hard or even engage in a meaningful prayer life if we as parents have lost these gifts ourselves through our addiction to the amusement of shooting tube.

TV Values—the Lowest Common Denominator

Karl Barth once said, "We have to challenge the right of this passing age to set the agenda for our lives." This is roughly equivalent to Paul's exhortation in Romans 12:2, "Do not conform any longer to the pattern of this world, but be transformed by the renewing of your mind." The basic principle is worldly garbage in, worldly garbage out. What we allow into our lives will determine who we become and how we live. Jesus taught us that "the eye is the lamp of the body. If your eyes are good, your whole body will be full of light. But if your eyes are bad, your whole body will be full of darkness" (Mt 6:22-23). We need to watch what we watch.

We are to guard against taking on the values of the world. Instead we are to experience a renewing of our minds so that we can influence the fallen world around us. We are to be salt and light in the world. Television has the power to invade our minds and overwhelm us with secular values. But for us as Christians, God's Word defines good and evil, right and wrong. God's revelation is an objective and normative standard for all humanity. Our obligation is to learn the truth and conform our lives to it.

The world's perspective is that men and women make subjective and autonomous judgments about values and that there is no objective standard that can be applied to all. Those who live by this believe they can take God's place in making pronouncements about what is true and good. But without God's guidance and with no absolute standards that apply to everyone, morality is an empty concept. Instead of moral guidance to live by and a standard to judge human behavior, values are no more than personal opinions with no basis beyond one's self. And nowhere does this happen with greater frequency and power than on television.

I remember watching one of the Academy Awards programs some time ago. I heard from three film personalities during the program that what we need in our world is more love and less hatred. Therefore, how can anyone today criticize a genuine love relationship between two people, even if the two happen to be of the same gender? If you and your children hear a hundred times or more that homosexual relationships are an expression of love between individuals that is "good," the message will begin to work its way into your worldview. Line by line this passing world shapes our perceptions of reality, adds its subjective shading to the moral agendas of our personal lives.

As Christians we need to be clear about what the Bible teaches.

[156]

We have to be active TV watchers, discussing together as a family what is coming into our living rooms on the tube. Otherwise we become desensitized to and molded by the world's agenda.

Over the past decade or so I have observed a tremendous shift in sexual values. Television creates fantasies that, in time, become the normative behaviors of the viewing public. This pattern has repeated itself over and over. F. A. Voigt once wrote, "The transition from things imagined to things real is a very easy one, and men, no less than children, will suit action to fantasy."[8] It is difficult to find a young person today—even a young believer strong in her faith—who can articulate a biblical position regarding why it would be wrong to have sex before marriage. It is becoming commonplace now for young people to show up for premarital counseling who share the same address. I cannot help but believe this proves the power of television and other media to transform moral consciousness.

Television often promotes a worldview that is in direct opposition to God's Word. Jesus said that "anyone who looks at a woman lustfully has already committed adultery with her in his heart" (Mt 5:28). Yet TV promotes adultery as an acceptable, and even desirable, cultural value. Television producers most often champion the minority views on issues like homosexuality, adultery and abortion rights. The danger here is what this incessant dripping of the humanist agenda can accomplish in the untrained minds of our young children and, over time, even in us as adult believers.

When television producers are not championing the values held by liberal minorities, they will probably be working hard at affirming other widely held beliefs of our culture. This is the safest place for commercial TV to be in the values arena. It has to attract large, heterogeneous audiences to have economic success. By and large people do not want to be changed. They want to be told that what they already believe is acceptable. "For the time will come," Paul wrote to Timothy, "when men will not put up with sound doctrine. Instead, to suit their own desires, they will gather around them a great number of teachers to say what their itching ears want to hear" (2 Tim 4:3). Television producers understand this aspect of human nature well. To quote Quentin Schultze again, "In commercial television, the drive for audience ratings leads to stories that confirm (support the cultural status quo). . . . Nearly all commercial TV series are trying to resonate with audience taste, not question existing values and beliefs."[9]

Basically, this means that commercial TV will seldom challenge you with a higher thought. It will reduce morality to the lowest common denominator. Commercial television will not raise our moral standards. It cannot afford to turn off the masses who, if offended, might turn off their sets. Stereotypes are confirmed. Sitcom after sitcom, soap after soap offers the same weak broth. Commercial television will not create a vision for a better life.

People in this world are starved for such a vision but do not know where to turn. As followers of Christ we need to offer the world this vision of life as it *could* be. God's Word can renew our minds, give us hope and transform our lives. And by the grace of God we can bring true healing to the hurting world around us. But TV will make us impotent to be change agents if we cannot break its claim on our time, our minds and our children's lives.

The TV Personality as Prophet

Television has the power to create an electronic personality, a visual image, to which we as viewers are drawn. Too often we find ourselves unwittingly pledging our political, moral, intellectual or economic allegiance to these contrived TV personalities. This even happens in Christian broadcasting. Church members will often give moderately to their home churches while being exceedingly generous to the ministry of a TV personality they have never met. (And the TV personality is never as accountable for those funds as the local church and pastor have to be.) All the while, many local churches and faithful pastors continue to struggle financially.

Well-meaning Christians buy into these TV ministries with their gut-wrenching promotional stories of changed lives. The TV evangelist is always dressed to the hilt. He is moved to tears at just the right moment. Then the camera zooms in on someone in the audience with tears streaming down her face. This irresistible persona is created in the privacy of your own home. But with your local pastor, things are different. Remember the time he made that offhand comment that offended you? Sure, it was eight years ago. But it has stuck with you. And last Sunday's sermon was weak again. Your pastor's message didn't even come close to the sermon the TV pastor delivered before you came to church.

The point is, there is no way the home pastor can match what is done on TV. Your pastor does not have the advantage of being able to use clever technology to enhance his image. He can't even get the board to put in some decent lighting up front so you can see his face on Sunday morning. You also live in the same community with your pastor and his family. You see your pastor operating in real life. He makes mistakes. He will occasionally say the wrong thing or promote something you would rather not see in your church. This aggravates you. So you send your money to a highly produced, intimate image that comes into your living room on cable. That's not smart. And it's not right.

The TV personality becomes a prophet in our culture if we uncritically accept what the image and personality tell us to believe. Take the powerful persona of Madonna with the younger audience. It is frightening when a twisted and self-consumed person like Madonna, by virtue of the fact that she has won an enormous amount of exposure in our culture (no pun intended), can speak out from her personal agenda with the force of prophetic utterance. Young people around the world who have surrendered their reason to the image lose their ability to evaluate the message. Even my daughter, Jana, who does not like Madonna's immorality and disrespect for Christianity, talks about how courageous she thinks Madonna is in expressing what she really believes. But this is part of Madonna's created persona. It is an element of her carefully crafted media personality. We need to stop for a second in our families and talk about the real meaning of courage. Then we can judge whether Madonna embodies that character trait. Television presents image over idea, personality over proposition. We buy in at the emotional level and too often fail to engage our minds regarding the image that is being projected.

Television can also create an intoxicating image of authentic character. A TV personality can come off as extraordinarily humble, caring and selfless. It hurts when we realize we have been taken in. Jim and Tammy Bakker took in millions of believing men and women—and took in millions of dollars too. Jimmy Swaggart was not what he appeared to be. We gobble up these TV and film personalities with little concern for the poison we may be ingesting along with the fine-looking fare.

The temptation to be like God is as strong today as it was for Adam and Eve in the Garden. TV can produce an image of godliness without the substance. Once we buy into the image, what the image says becomes convincing. When the images speak to us in our living rooms, we need to be very careful about what is being said, whether it comes from the lips of Hillary Clinton or the beak of Big Bird.

Steps Toward Recovery

I was listening to Christian radio while driving a few days ago and heard an appeal from CLEAR TV, a Christian-based organization dedicated to clearing from television its most offensive elements. Based on the organization's strategy of going after the advertisers, the spokesperson was calling for a boycott of a major company with a long track record of supporting the wrong kinds of programs. I was in favor of the boycott and agreed with CLEAR TV about the offensive nature of most of the shows listed. The problem was, I really like a couple of the shows that CLEAR TV had decided should be off limits. The question became an issue of integrity for me. How can I support a boycott against an advertiser if I am not willing to stop watching the programs in question?

My guess is that there are probably thousands of Christian men and women who will support the boycott, but in the privacy of their own homes will continue to watch some of the popular programs on CLEAR TV's hit list (or other programs of questionable value). If we are not willing to make tough choices about what we will watch and how much we watch, commercial TV will continue to produce the same kinds of programs.

Our personal and family choices about TV watching reflect our willingness to take a stand for righteous living in our day. We do a lot of talking about right living, but practicing what we preach is much harder than voicing our opinions. Are we serious about living out our commitments?

We never had cable TV in our home until we moved to northern California a few years ago. We found out quickly that because of the hills that surrounded our home, it was impossible to get any reception of regular channels. We had to sign on with the cable company if we wanted to view television programs in our home. We chose not to accept any of the movie channel options. I knew that I would have trouble controlling what I watched and even more trouble monitoring the kids' choices. Judie and I also believed that it was going to be hard enough to help our four teenagers make good decisions about movies without having every new film coming right into our home.

A day or two after the cable was installed I ran across the Playboy channel. It was scrambled, but the sound was active. I experienced a temptation to return to the channel later. The next day I called the cable company and asked if the scrambled channel could be removed from the signals coming into our home. Someone came out that day and cut off the signal completely. We all need to be tough on ourselves and honest about our temptations to watch programs that are not helpful to us and not honoring to our commitment to Christ.

It has been an ongoing struggle for Judie and me to decide with our children what television programs or videos are worth watching. We often disagree with each other. Judie is turned off by profanity of any kind. I usually argue that some profanity can be ignored if the content of the dramatic production is strong and worthwhile (we no longer have young children at home). In discussions with our teenagers, we wrestle over the appropriateness of sexuality and violence as they are portrayed on TV. We have found it nearly impossible to set absolute rules with which we can all be comfortable.

One of our family's favorite films is *The Mission,* a story of Spanish and Portuguese conquests in South America and a few priests who tried to save an Indian mission at San Miguel. There is nudity in the film. Our family agrees that it is not in the least prurient. In fact, we watched the modified version on prime-time television one night and thought that what was cut to eliminate the nudity ruined the overall quality of atmosphere and honesty in presenting an authentic picture of that early Indian culture. Our family will continue to wrestle with our choices, but the struggle is good and profitable. Dialoguing with one another over questions of morality is very helpful as we challenge each other's views and try to take a stand that promotes artistic honesty, recognizes the quality of acting and producing, and supports themes that help us to learn and grow.

Of course, all along the way there are choices that have to be made regarding what younger children should see and hear. Judie and I are often astonished at what parents today will allow into the lives of their young children. When our kids were younger, invitations to birthday parties often included games and videos. We had to ask ahead of time what movies were going to be shown. We often found ourselves involved in gracious conversations with other parents about their video choices. Most of the time the discussions were profitable. Sometimes they were not, and we had to explain to our children why we could not allow them to attend.

[162]

We have always believed that the best way to help our kids be discerning themselves is to continue this ongoing dialogue regarding values and tastes. Some of our friends have chosen the all-or-nothing route with TV. They just do not have one in their home. If this works, it may be the best solution for some. But we have not found that this has worked very well in the lives of our friends who have tried it. A friend of our daughter, Jana, whose parents had no TV, turned into a kind of TV junkie through her deprivation. When she came over to our house to play with Jana, she wanted to do nothing but watch TV. We believe it is better to have a television and teach kids how to be discerning about it than to create a fascination and hunger for the experience without educating them on how to handle it.

There are other choices we should be making. Judie found that it had become a habit with her to turn on the television as she worked around the house. She told me later that she realized how this can lead to indiscriminate viewing of anything that happens to be on at the time. So she quit doing it. It is also good to be conscious of where your television is positioned in the family room or living room. Is it the focus of the room? The very positioning of the TV set can determine how much it is used. One of our family rules is to keep the television off during mealtimes. Our family dining area connects the kitchen with the family room, and it is easy to have the TV on while we eat. But this destroys the best opportunity for family interaction we have during the day. We have learned to keep the TV off.

The number of televisions you have in your home also contributes to the amount of TV viewing you do as a family. If we had it to do over again, we would choose to have one television. This would force us to decide *as a family* what to watch and what not to watch. The convenience of having a second or even third television adds to isolated individual viewing with less accountability to one another in the family.

Young families would do well to choose to watch programs

together. We should watch programs, not watch TV. We easily get into lazy grazing, sitting for hours in front of the TV just to pass the time. We can use our VCRs to tape high-quality TV programs in order to create a home video library. This way we will be less dependent on what is currently offered. Our church library has a large and growing video section. I see a lineup of young families there every Sunday morning to check out good children's videos and family videos to watch during the week. We need to support and encourage our churches in this direction. I still like the "No TV Night" idea, where a family agrees to leave the TV off altogether at least one night a week. That commitment can provide opportunities for rich family time—singing, playing games, reading books together, riding bikes, strolling through the park or just talking around a big bowl of popcorn.[10]

TV Literacy—Learning How to Watch

Cultural analyst Os Guinness made up a game with his son, Christopher, who was five years old at the time. He called the game "Spot the Lie." He wanted his son to learn how to discern the truth from sham in television commercials. When a TV commercial came on, Os would say, "Spot the lie." His son would then try to discover the irrational statement, the false sense of reality or which clever technique was being used to manipulate. If his son found something, Os would give him a quarter for his efforts. Os says, "Before Christopher bankrupted me, he grew disillusioned with what he was seeing on television. He's eleven now, and he much prefers to read novels and do other things. Most of what's on TV doesn't measure up to his standards."[11]

We all need to learn how to spot the lies in both commercials and regular programming. Television is a major part of our modern lives, and we need to learn as much as we can about how the media uses visual images and sound. Bill Moyers once said, "I think young people are going to have to be taught visual literacy in the same way I was taught . . . to diagram sentences."[12] As

[164]

regular TV viewers, we need to understand the power and technique of visual imagery. If we can become more visually literate, we will be less susceptible to manipulation by the television media and better at judging the quality of a program. We will become more demanding about what is offered, and this is what TV needs.

You may want to start a Sunday-school class in your church where fellow believers can discuss the use of television today. Together you can watch commercials, dramatic presentations and sitcoms, followed up by group discussion and critique. You may want to ask questions like the following:

☐ What seemed realistically done in the program? What was not realistic?

☐ How different is your family from the one pictured in the sitcom? Compare and contrast. Which family do you like best, and why?

☐ If you were the producer of this show, what would you have done differently?

☐ What technique did the commercials use to urge you to purchase certain things or accept certain attitudes?

☐ What technical or visual realities were operating powerfully in the program or in this commercial?[13]

We can also actively encourage private and public schools to become more involved in teaching visual literacy to our children. After all, our schools are dedicated to helping young people be informed and skilled for living in the contemporary world. And television is a major influence in our contemporary world. Certainly learning how to view television is a critically important learning goal for young people today. Public schools will respond to this request if we emphasize that it is learning how to manage the media and evaluate its technical events that is our main concern.

Of course, we are best equipped for evaluating what we see and hear from the tube if we are biblically literate. If we want to make informed judgments as parents, we need to think and act from a biblical base. If you have not taken your biblical education seriously as parents, this has to be a first priority for you. Then you will be able to disciple your children. Without this Christian foundation in your life you will be trying to make ethical decisions with no normative standard to guide you. Be a biblical disciple of Christ and you will have something to offer your family members as they question these important issues. And you will also have a solid life foundation to offer direction to a lost and searching world.

The Larger Vision

I have wondered why the programs I watch on the Christian television channel are often poorly done. Perhaps our evangelical Christian culture has been so strongly antitelevision that we have turned our gifted young people away from thinking about and pursuing careers in the television industry. We need a new vision for television that combines strong moral integrity with equally strong creative integrity to produce programs that redefine what television can be and do in our culture. In order to accomplish this, we have to encourage our gifted young people to enter the television industry and to live out their Christian commitment to integrity through acting, producing, editing and even advertising. I believe it can happen. I have not given up hope that good things can be accomplished in the future of commercial television.

In the meantime we can become more informed about what is already offered on the public broadcasting networks. Spread the word about family programs of interest, and be willing to financially support public broadcasting that is doing a good job of offering worthwhile alternatives to commercial television. You will not agree with everything you see on PBS. But the quality of public television productions and the honest way they approach various points of view is refreshing when compared to the content of the vast majority of commercial TV productions. Commercial TV has to cater far more to the tastes of the lowest common denominator in the viewing public. The more we support public broadcasting, the freer these networks are to choose and produce programs purely on the basis of their cultural and artistic merit.

The longer I study this issue, the more convinced I am becoming that more government regulation is needed, especially regarding what will be shown during prime time. This is another way we can work for change. Americans can encourage the FCC to take a stronger role in making guidelines for prime-time viewing on commercial television.

There was a long period in the sixties and seventies when the effect of television on young people was studied in depth. The results were not surprising. Accumulated research pointed to a "pattern of positive association between the viewing of television violence and aggressive attitudes and behavior" in children.[14] The FCC came up with a number of voluntary guidelines and suggestions to help the industry manage itself. None of these good suggestions worked.

Broadcasters also found out that the FCC was going to require a minimum of seven and a half hours a week of age-appropriate children's programs. But before the networks could respond, the Reagan administration took office, with a strong bias against regulation. By 1984 the FCC had removed virtually all guidelines on program content and had abolished any regulations previously in force that put limitations on the kind of advertising that can accompany children's programs. This is one of the major reasons we now have *Jenny Jones, Ricki Lake* and *Geraldo* after school and during prime-time viewing. A third of the viewers who watch these programs are children under thirteen.

The predominant content of these programs is crime, violence and sex (often deviant sex). For example, in November of 1989 *Geraldo* ran programs on serial rapists, pregnant prison inmates, teenage prostitution, nymphomaniacs, and rape on college campuses. Think of the impression being formed in the minds of the millions of children watching these shows without parental supervision. Kids are introduced to a dangerous, sex-craved, violent world, where anything goes and no one really cares anymore about right or wrong, good or bad. And the worst people seem to make out like bandits selling their stories on talk shows. This is just one example of what deregulation has led to in American broadcasting.[15]

If American televisions are turned on six to seven hours a day, and the average grade-school child spends more time in front of the TV than in school, shouldn't the FCC be more concerned about what is broadcast during prime-time hours? Doesn't it seem wise to take advantage of the prime afternoon hours to produce programming that is beneficial to children? And shouldn't there be regulations in place to guide how products are advertised and what kinds of products can be advertised on these children's programs? This kind of regulation works in Britain, Australia and Japan. It can work for Americans too. Even if you are politically opposed to heavy government regulation, you can see what deregulation has led to in the TV industry. Children today are virtually at the mercy of the private market, which is driven solely by economic concerns. This is getting us nowhere.[16]

Those of us who like to write letters should send them to the FCC and the White House. We need to urge our government to regulate the television industry closely and fund projects aimed at improving children's programming. We can also write letters to producers and networks when they do the right thing. So often we write negative letters when we are disturbed. How about catching networks doing something right and praising them for it?

Is Television a Trojan Horse?

The ancient Greek city of Troy was given a gift—a huge wooden horse. It looked harmless, but hidden inside were soldiers ready to destroy the city. Similarly, television seemed so harmless to us all in its infancy. It was a new form of entertainment that looked like it would only improve our lives. But now we know firsthand its seductive power. We might be tempted to destroy our televisions before they destroy us. But this may be a case of throwing the baby out with the bathwater.

Let's not give up hope, not yet. Let's focus on our families first, making choices that reflect our values and that teach our children to be discerning in their choices. Then let's look for opportunities to make a difference, whether supporting public broadcasting, teaching a Sunday-school class on television viewing, writing letters to the networks and the government on a regular basis, praying daily for healthy changes or supporting a Christian young person's choice to enter the television industry.

I am not ready to give it up. Admittedly, television has enormous potential for evil, but it has an equally enormous potential for good. Like everything else in God's creation, it is how it is used that makes all the difference. As Christians, we can conceive of a new tele-*vision*. This new vision will require us to choose wisely the programs we watch, to work toward improving Christian programming and to commit ourselves to influencing the future of television for Christ.

It will be our personal commitment to change and our willingness to take action that will finally determine whether this large-screen box becomes a Trojan horse that destroys our families or a powerful tool to enhance our learning and growing together.

Questions for Discussion

1. The author believes that there are many similarities between the television-watching experience and the drug experience. Discuss together his statement on page 150, "Young people are being trained [by TV] in addictive behavior before they're even old enough to know what drugs are."

2. How much time is given to watching television in your family? If the televisions were suddenly taken out of your home, how do you think your family would use the time gained? Do you think that after the shock wore off, having no TV would be a positive

thing for your family? Why or why not?

3. The author suggests several things that can be wrong with television viewing:

a. Television viewing is passive and discourages rational interaction.

b. Television often presents a superficial view of life that does not prepare us to manage life as it really is.

c. Television generally affirms the values held by the culture and often promotes a worldview that is in direct opposition to the values of biblical Christianity.

d. Television can create an intoxicating image of authentic character, and naive viewers can be conned by it.

Do you think these are valid criticisms of the television medium? How will these insights influence what your family watches on TV, and how you watch it?

4. What decisions has your family made to try to manage television viewing time? What has worked? What has not worked? What are some new ideas from this chapter that you might want to put into practice in your home?

11
Tempted to Forget the Love

•

One day Judie received a call from Jason's middle-school English teacher. The teacher asked if Judie and I could come in to see her. They set up a time. The teacher did not say why she wanted to meet with us, and we were a little nervous going in.

Jason's teacher met us, invited us to sit down and then explained that she wanted to talk with us about a speech Jason had given. He and others were to talk on the topic "Life's Greatest Gift." She explained that when Jason gave his speech, she was reduced to tears in the back of the room. She had his notes typed up so we could have a copy. The following is the speech Jason gave to his seventh-grade class:

Once, when I was a lot younger, I watched a television show on abortion. I saw how many thousands of women were aborting their babies before their babies were born. I remember how glad I was that my biological mother chose to carry me and my twin brother, Josh, full term and give birth. Then she let us be adopted into a wonderful family.

I might not even be here today. But my biological mother loved me enough to let me be born. And my new family loved me enough to make a wonderful home for me. This is why I think adoption is the greatest gift.

A lot of people might think being adopted is a bad thing. They think maybe the parents that adopt you might not love you as much as their own kids. Sometimes this is true, but in my family it is not.

The reason I say this is because my parents who adopted me were taking a very high risk. They knew in my biological family there was a problem known as dyslexia, a severe reading disability. They also knew there was diabetes in my biological family. We were also born with one foot turned in, and I had to have surgery to correct an indentation in my skull. They knew they would need to give me special attention.

Knowing all this, they still wanted us; even as twins with twice the work. My mom and dad didn't care that we were black and they were white. They loved us just the way we were.

There are a lot of things I like about being adopted. First, we know where we belong. We are not like kids in foster homes that get moved around a lot. Another good thing about adoption is that I know I was chosen. Some kids might not know if they were wanted or not. But I can always be sure that I was really wanted. I was chosen. The last thing I like about being adopted is being in this family. We are brought up in a good, loving Christian family.

I think my biological mom probably likes the idea that we are adopted. She could not take care of us. She and my biological father did not want to get married. By giving us up for adoption, my mother knew we would have a father and a mother who could take care of us with good housing and schooling. When I get to be eighteen years old, I know I could look for my biological parents, but I won't. I already have a loving and caring mom and dad.

Adoption is the greatest gift in life.

Adoption was God's idea first. It is God's way of including us in *his* family. It is his way of showing us in no uncertain terms that he is serious about showering us with love, his special kind of love—unconditional love. The apostle Paul writes, "For he [God] chose us in him [Jesus] before the creation of the world. . . . In love he predestined us to be adopted as his sons through Jesus Christ, in accordance with his pleasure and will—to the praise of his glorious grace, which he has freely given us in the One he loves" (Eph 1:4-6).

Love, unconditional love, is the lifeblood of family relationships. What was touching to us in Jason's speech was how clearly he was able to state what unconditional love is all about—"They loved us just the way we were." Judie and I do not feel we deserve the accolades Jason heaped on us in his speech. Our three adopted children and our biological child have blessed our lives far more than we will ever be a blessing to them. But we were both deeply thankful that in the midst of all our floundering as parents, and with the many mistakes in judgment we've made in our family along the way, God was still able to work through us as Christian parents. The most important thing we wanted to communicate to our children was that they are loved unconditionally.

Our primary goal as Christian parents will always be to find as many ways as we can—verbally and nonverbally—to let each child know: *there is nothing you can ever do to make me love you more; there is nothing you could ever do to make me love you less.* This is agape love. It is the love God the Father has for his Son, "the One he loves." And God showed each of us this kind of love by choosing us and, with great pleasure, adopting us into his family. It is a wonderful thing to grow up in a family where you feel chosen and loved.

Love Means Supporting and Encouraging Individuality

Judie came to me one day when our children were still very young and told me she thought I was tougher on Gabe than I was on the rest of the kids. We have four children: Jana, Jason and Josh are

[173]

adopted; Gabe, our biological child, is the youngest.

At first I had a hard time believing that Judie's perception could be true. Then, as I watched myself more carefully, I saw that she was right. I was harder on Gabe. It seemed that with the three adopted children I was willing to allow them complete freedom related to their gifts and interests and what they wanted to do. It was easy for me to create space for the adopted kids. I was able to let the real person emerge in a natural way. I felt free to affirm what I saw developing. But with Gabe, I had a plan for his life. Judie observed how I withheld affirmation from Gabe if his choices and behavior did not coincide with my preconceived notions about who he ought to be and how he should be developing as my son.

Our biological children are a kind of judgment on our genes. The level of success they achieve says something about who I am as a parent and a father. Therefore it's hard to relax. We can become too controlling and manipulative, too involved in directing our children's future. I have known families where it is fine for sons to be athletes, but if one of the boys takes up guitar, his father is displeased and withholds love. I have known other families where it is fine for the children to follow their interests in music, but if one of the kids develops an interest in athletics, her parents turn away from her emotionally. We often give the strong message to our kids that we can't love them unless they become doctors or lawyers or dancers or take over the family business. This is conditional love.

Do you have a compelling dream about what you believe your son or daughter should become? If you love your dream more than you love your real daughter or son, your dream will destroy your child. We need instead to watch for the real person to emerge, and to be quick to encourage the potential we see. This does not mean that we shrink back from discussing with our children the positives and negatives of different life and vocational choices. But we are most interested in identifying the individual strengths and gifts that God has created in our sons and daughters. Each God-given gift can be developed in a variety of ways (1 Cor 12:4-6). Become skilled at naming and aiming your children's gifts and potential areas of strength.

You would think that I learned my lesson back then and now would not have to watch myself as carefully. But a few months ago Gabe told me he was thinking about attending a trade school to learn auto mechanics instead of going to college. My response was condescending, and it hurt him: "Why would you want to do a thing like that?"

Gabe is a gifted artist. He's been in advanced art since his sophomore year in high school. At this time in his life, though, he's become very interested in auto mechanics, and he's good at it. Again, we can talk with our children about the pros and cons of different career choices, but a comment like mine strongly suggests that I believe some vocations are inherently superior or inferior to others. This is wrong.

Love Means Quantity Time Together

We hear so much today about spending "quality time" with spouses and children. The idea that quality time will suffice when it is impossible to find periods of quantity time together is a myth. You simply cannot program a quality relational event to occur in a fifteen-minute block of time. Quality family times cannot be scheduled or forced. They happen most often during longer periods of relaxed time together.

A favorite source of uninterrupted time for me has been family vacations when we were all trapped together in the car for hours. While Judie drove, I would crawl in the back and talk, horse around and generally have fun. But all of a sudden we'd be into something really good; in-depth sharing was taking place. This will never happen if you take twenty minutes of "quality" time at the end of a day and try to *make it happen*. We need to find ways of spending quantity time together so the truly quality moments will

[175]

happen often in our families.

Quality times will often emerge while you're working together as a family. I've enjoyed the times Gabe and I have had recently rebuilding the engine in his car. We've had hours and hours together we might not have gotten in any other way. The same thing happened with all three boys a couple of years back when we took out trees in the back yard and put in a basketball court.

Set aside special times for each child. And schedule a weekly date time for Mom and Dad. Protect family time around all the holidays. Don't forget what good times can be had when you read together and talk about the stories you read. At a family meeting ask the kids about their favorite times together as a family. Then reschedule these same kinds of events as family times together in the near future.

Love Means Having Fun Together as a Family

Is there joy in your home? Do you often find yourselves just laughing out loud with each other? Having fun together builds love and lasting memories. It would be great if when asked what it was like to grow up in a Christian home, our kids answered, "I'll tell you what it's like. We had fun!"

My mom had a gift for turning moments of disaster into family fun. One time in particular stands out in my memory. We grew up on a farm in Wisconsin. The farmhouse had a huge kitchen with a linoleum floor. One modern convenience in the kitchen was a dishwasher. One summer afternoon the dishwasher exploded, and water and suds shot out all over the kitchen. The kitchen floor was transformed into a lake of hot, soapy water.

My mom yelled, "Get your swimming suits!" For the next hour we took turns running through the living room, diving into the kitchen and sliding across the soapy kitchen floor. We had the time of our lives. My mom told all of her friends how great it was not to have to scrub that week.

I heard another story of a family whose vacation plans were

suddenly ruined by the dad's boss, who insisted that Dad meet and entertain a visiting team of corporate consultants. The father didn't want to change the family's scheduled vacation. They had mapped out everything so carefully together—the routes they were going to take, where they were going to stay and what they were going to see and do.

A few days before the family was scheduled to leave, the visiting team of consultants changed their plans. Dad was free to go now. But he didn't tell anyone. He said goodby to all the family members and played it straight. He had already arranged a short flight for the next day and a ride that would take him to a spot on the highway he knew the family car would have to pass. He waited there until he saw them coming, then walked out onto the shoulder and stuck his thumb out. You can imagine the shock and then the fun when they saw their dad, the hitchhiker, with his thumb out and a big smile on his face. Then they had the joy of spending the rest of their vacation time together.

One young family we love plans a "Rude Night" every once in a while. The kids don't have to follow the usual family rules of etiquette at the dinner table, like saying "please" and "thank you." They decide together what they want for their special meal and then eat with their fingers. The kids are all given straws so they can blow bubbles in their milk. There's only one rule: no throwing food. These creative, fun times make memories that are joyfully relived in family reminiscing throughout the years.

Tom and Judie's Morning Prayer When the Kids Were Little

Tom and Judie: Dear God, thank you that we have survived another day and night, and for this new day beginning. Give us this day an extra measure of your grace and love.

Judie: Grant me self-control this morning when I leave the kitchen for only a second and baby Gabe spoons half his Cheerios on the floor and puts the rest of the bowl upside-down on his head for a hat. And later, Lord, give me patience when Jana balks at potty training and three minutes later wets in my lap.

Tom: And let me know, Lord, when I'm lying on the floor laughing out loud, tossing Jana gently up and down, and she throws up in my mouth, that all things work together for good for those who love you.

Judie: Help me, Father, to accept graciously the gifts of love all the kids bring me: the sun-dried toads, the flattened grasshoppers, the drowned roly-polies, the live wasp grasped by one wing, spiders dangling from one mangled leg, and hosts of dandelions and other dead weeds drooping out of the top of the neighbor's old dog-food cans.

Tom: And Father, help me to appreciate boyish curiosity when I find Gabe's peanut butter sandwich stuffed into the holes of the electric motor on my new radial arm saw.

Judie: And me too, Father, when I'm working with tweezers to remove all the raisins Joshua stuck up Gabe's nose.

Tom: I want to be thankful, Lord—really—that Gabe wasn't cut to shreds when he smashed the grasshopper on the picture window with a boulder.

Judie: Dear Father, help me to accept your lessons in humility when Jana cuts gobs of hair from the neighbor girl's head, and later I see Jason with his pants down going potty in the middle of the street.

Tom: And give Judie a sense of humor, Lord, when we're late for church and frantically searching for little Gabe, only to find him downstairs, dressed in his new virgin wool, light beige outfit from Grandma, sitting at the back of the fireplace tossing ashes over his head and clothes. Help us both to smile back at the little white smile that shines forth from the darkness.

Judie: And Father, at mealtimes give us both grateful hearts for a family with sturdy digestive systems, a family that can actually enjoy eating in an environment of utter chaos. Give me patience, Lord, when the kids look at my new casserole and say, "What's *that?*" And let me remain calm when Jason spills his milk all over the table, and it runs into my shoe. I regret sounding pessimistic, Lord, but you've been to our house at mealtimes. You know how it is.

Tom: I pray that when Judie runs back into the supermarket to redeem the thirty-five-cent coupon she'd forgotten in the rush, and comes back to find Gabe stomping around with three dozen smashed eggs under his feet in the front seat, she won't go insane. Give her the strength it takes to be a loving Christian mother.

Judie: And I pray for Tom's sake that when he comes home after people have been chinning themselves on his nerves all day, I can remain somewhat composed for at least ten minutes before breaking down and unloading on him.

Tom and Judie: And dear God, together we ask you to help us pray at the end of each and every day without gritting our teeth. For the quiet moments at bedtime, Father, we are truly grateful. Amen and amen.

Love Means Plenty of Hugging and Kissing

Do you hug and hold your sons and daughters? Men will sometimes make the mistake of only wrestling with their sons, but never hugging, kissing and holding them. Both sons and daughters need to be shown this kind of affectionate love.

As boys and girls explore their new identities during preadolescence and into the teen years, there will be changes. Young boys may tell their moms at some point that hugs are okay, but not kisses. Daughters who are developing physically need the freedom to find new boundaries with their fathers that are natural and appropriate for them. But there are always healthy and natural ways to express our love through touching, even if it's just standing with an arm around a teenage son or daughter, or giving a simple pat on the back. Many kids return to hugs and kisses with Mom and Dad after they are comfortable with who they are as adult men and women. We need to let them go through this natural process of finding out who they are at each new stage.

My friend Joe told me about the painful experience he and his son Tim went through when Tim was in his late teens. Tim left home. The family relationship was broken. Tim moved in with others his own age in a little flat in Chicago. One night Joe was awakened from sleep by a phone call. A voice he did not recognize said, "Mr. Bayly, your son Tim has been in a terrible accident. He has been taken to the emergency room . . ." And then the line went dead.

Joe jumped out of bed. He first called the police, who did not have any record of an accident or emergency situation involving Tim Bayly. Joe rushed out to a hospital nearby, but Tim had not been admitted there. Then Joe went to a hospital in the area where Tim was living. They also had no record of anyone by that name being admitted through emergency. Joe called several other hospitals and got the same response.

Still frantic with worry, Joe finally went to the apartment where he knew Tim was staying. He went up the stairs from the street. The door was open. He walked in. There were several young people sleeping on the floor in sleeping bags. Joe could see by the dim light coming in from the street that Tim was there, asleep on the floor. Joe's grief and frustration turned into a father's tears of joy. He just knelt quietly on the floor next to his son, leaned over, kissed him gently on the side of his face, got up and walked out.

The next day one of Tim's young friends said to him, "Tim, did I ever get your dad good last night." He went on to tell Tim about the call in the middle of the night. Tim knew his dad had been there. He knew his dad had kissed him on the cheek. Now it all came clear to him. Within the week Tim and Joe were talking again. Tim knew without a doubt by what had happened that his father loved him. Like the prince whose kiss awoke Sleeping Beauty to new life, this father bent over his son and with a kiss blessed into life a new relationship. The relationship had looked irreparable before. But now love and forgiveness flowed between them.

Love Means Asking Forgiveness

Two of the hardest words we ever have to say are "I'm sorry." They are so hard to say because we have to die a little bit each time we say them. We have to put a part of ourselves to death to say "I'm sorry" and really mean it. We put to death our pride, our need to be right, our coveted image. It is hard to accept responsibility for our mistakes and put things right by asking forgiveness.

As parents we need to model a forgiving spirit. Asking to be forgiven is at the heart of living life as a Christian man or woman. It is the God-ordained means by which we are given the gift of right relationship with Christ. And it is the God-ordained means by which we maintain right relationships within our families. As parents we will find it easy to tell our children to say they are sorry. But we will find it harder to ask for forgiveness and tell our children *we* are sorry when we have been in the wrong.

There are many times that Judie and I have had to ask forgiveness of our kids. I remember one time when Jana was junior-high age and had some friends over. They were talking together about their classes at school as I walked through the room. Without thinking I made a comment to the group about Jana's poor showing in math, her hardest subject. In an instant I saw her eyes well up with tears.

Later I went to her room. I told her, "I'm sorry for what I said to you tonight in front of your friends. I know that hurt you. I will never do that again if I can help it. Will you forgive me?"

Jana said, "It's okay, Dad."

I said, "No, it's not. I need your forgiveness. Will you forgive me?"

"I forgive you, Dad," she said.

Our homes should be places where forgiveness is granted willingly and eagerly, and never withheld. Forgiveness is a gift we should all give and receive often. It frees us from having to be perfect in order to be loved. And forgiveness keeps relationships intact and brings healing to broken relationships before bitterness and anger have time to set in.

An incident happened recently that showed me I still have room to grow in this area. Judie and I had a tough time with some issue one night a couple of months ago. It was late when I left her in the family room and crawled in bed alone. Our problem was not resolved. I was lying in bed, thinking. I was still angry. I remembered the scriptural admonition from the apostle Paul, "Do not let the sun go down while you are still angry" (see Eph 4:26). I thought, *Well, I better do something here.* Then I said to myself, *Wait. The sun is already down. I've got until tomorrow night!*

Fortunately for both of us, Judie came in at that moment. She demonstrated the maturity I wish I had displayed by asking if we couldn't put this behind us. We both said we were sorry and had a time of prayer together to set things straight.

I like the description I once heard that a good marriage is a romance in which the hero and heroine both die in the first chapter.

Love Means Verbally Encouraging and Affirming One Another

The apostle Paul writes, "Do not let any unwholesome talk come out of your mouths, but only what is helpful for building others up according to their needs, that it may benefit those who listen" (Eph 4:29). In our families we should be in the business of trying to catch someone doing something right and affirming these things whenever we see them.

I remember once talking to a woman who struggled with deep feelings of inadequacy. I asked if her husband affirmed her often. She said, "Never." I asked if she had talked with him about it. She said she'd asked him if he would please tell her when she did things he appreciated, when she did something right. He had responded abruptly, "If you ever do anything right, I'll tell you!"

It would help us all to ask ourselves before speaking, *Will this build the other person up or tear the person down?* I have often thought it would be good to have a tape-recording system in every household so families could check up on their communication style. This way we could count how many times we have affirmed each other in our family in a day and compare it to how many times family members have been criticized by others. My guess is that in many of our homes the critical comments would far outweigh the affirmations. It ought to be the other way around. People will make positive changes in their lives much faster by being affirmed when they do things right than by being criticized when they do things wrong. When we need to correct, it is good to do this one on one, in private.

Focusing our attention on weaknesses is counterproductive. We should always emphasize the strengths in others and affirm these strengths. Then from this solid, positive base we can work on building new and complementary strengths.

I remember talking to a friend who told me how she managed to run her car into a ditch in a snowstorm. She said she had been worried all along about going into the ditch. As she became more and more anxious, her eye became fixed on the ditch. Finally she just drove the car right over the edge and down the embankment.

This same kind of thing can happen emotionally to our children or spouse if we constantly call attention to their weaknesses. They focus so intently on their weaknesses that they begin to fail and stutter in their areas of strength. But if we emphasize their strengths and capabilities, we have a good chance of bringing any weak areas up to the level of the current strengths. Authentic success in one area will bring about success in other areas of life. Affirmation is the power that makes this work. It is the power of love.

We have found that kids will pick up this skill if there is a positive flavor to the home environment. Jana used to leave affirming notes for her brothers. If you asked Josh who was the best in sports, he would say Jason was the best in soccer, Gabe in baseball, and his best sport was basketball. Kids learn the habit of finding something good to say.

Love Means Discipling Our Children

It has been said that we are in a kind of relay race in our Christian families. We take the baton from our parents if they were believers, and we are in the process of passing it on to our children. We are preparing them, with God's help, to accept Christ as Savior and Lord, to live a Christian life and, in time, to pass on our Christian beliefs and heritage to their children.

I once put together a course on the stages of family life for David C. Cook Publishing Company. From my research on that project, I learned that the majority of time churches today give to evangelism is spent sharing the gospel with kids who grew up in Christian homes but never really met Christ.

Discipleship happens best when we simply live out authentic Christianity on a daily basis. Deuteronomy 6:6-7 says, "These commandments that I give you today are to be upon your hearts. Impress them on your children. Talk about them when you sit at home and when you walk along the road, when you lie down and when you get up."

The key words here are *talk* and *impress*. We are to talk with and teach our children about the Lord. We do this best by being available to answer their questions. This beautiful little passage suggests that we will have times to sit down with our children, to walk with them, and that we will be there when they get up and when they go to bed. These are opportune times to reflect with our children on what it means to have Jesus in their lives. But we also have to *model* Christian living to our children, to *impress* upon them the truths of the Christian life. We do make an impression. We leave the stamp of authentic faith on the lives of our children when we believe it, live it, love it and demonstrate that we are willing to make deep sacrifices to live out the truth we claim.

The family is a planned community, designed by God, for the purpose of discipleship. In the family God has given us, we have the wonderful opportunity of working long-term in a small group setting, sharing our lives, our love and our thoughts. God knows that Christian character is built in hundreds of small, authentic steps. Our children hear the truth, but they also catch it in the same way they learn to speak. We teach some specific words to our young children, but most of their language is simply picked up by being around us when we speak. In a similar way, our kids are exposed to our faith every moment of the day—when we sit at home, when we walk along the road, when we lie down, when we get up.

How do we, for instance, most effectively teach our kids the importance of caring for God's creation? We talk about what the Bible teaches, but we also teach it by what we do with our garbage when we are at the lake, by what we do with our disposable diapers. We teach it by how many fish we take when they're really biting. Do we take more than our limit? We teach it by the care we take in putting out our fire when camping.

I remember watching our little guys when they were only about three feet tall, walking along ahead of us at Left Hand Reservoir in Colorado, picking up bottle caps and cans and sticking them in their packs and pockets to carry them out. For a parent it's gratifying to see that something is getting through, that something important to you as a Christian has made an impression on the lives of your children.

This is our primary task as Christian parents: to pass on a genuine Christian faith to our kids so that they will have an authentic relationship with Jesus. In turn, they will carry the gospel into the world in which they live, to their friends, classmates, acquaintances, coworkers and, ultimately, into their families, as they marry and have children of their own. If this discipleship does not happen, we have missed the most important thing.

I will open my mouth in parables,
   I will utter hidden things, things from of old—
what we have heard and known,
   what our fathers have told us.
We will not hide them from their children;

we will tell the next generation
the praiseworthy deeds of the LORD,
his power, and the wonders he has done. (Ps 78:2-4)

Love Means Reaching Out as a Family

One of our tasks as Christian parents should be to teach and train our children about their responsibility to others, so that they can make a difference in the lives of others. With so many pressures and commitments that erode family time, we become very protective of our time, and we should be. But if we're not careful, we can become enmeshed as a family, spending all of our free time doing things with and for our family while forgetting about the rest of the world around us. If this is the case, our children may begin to get the idea that our family is the only thing that matters in this world.

Some of our richest family times have been occasions when we have done outreach ministry together or taken vacation time to go on a short-term mission trip. Judie was instrumental very early in getting us involved as a family in ministry to others. She worked for a while as an aide in a nursing home. Judie saw many men and women there who were utterly alone in the world. They never went anywhere, because there was no one to take them. They never had anyone visit. We decided to start taking these folks out of the nursing home and with us to church or on picnics, or just into our home for an evening meal. We lived far away from grandparents at the time, and our daughter, Jana, especially enjoyed being with all these new grandmas and grandpas. We enjoyed being a surrogate family for these lovely older men and women who either had no family or had families that only neglected and ignored them.

Later, when we lived in Boulder, Colorado, the church there held an annual Thanksgiving feast for anyone who had no place else to go. The church fellowship hall filled up with street people, singles, the homeless, and university students who were alone on Thanksgiving. This is the earliest time I can remember when we took our very young children into a setting where we worked and served together with others to do something worthwhile for people who would have otherwise been alone or gone hungry. Our four children helped carry food to the tables and were surprisingly good at talking with these strangers, most of whom did not look or smell at all like people the kids came in contact with on a daily basis. This Thanksgiving outreach was a blessing for all of us. We would go home and have our family dinner later in the day, and it was amazing when we shared thanksgiving prayers how easy it was to identify God's blessings to us and to feel truly thankful as a family.

Judie and I have also taken one or more of the children with us when we have gone on short-term mission trips. The first trip we did as a family was to Lily of the Valley Home for Girls in San Lucas, Guatemala. Our children learned so much from the girls at the home. They learned about abuse and neglect in the lives of the kids who lived there. And they saw what a loving Christian environment, good food and good education can do to make a difference in someone's life. On this trip there was a lot of hard work to do, digging ditches and breaking up concrete. We worked as a team with other families to provide more electricity for the home and make needed improvements. There is a warm, good feeling that you have when you work hard together as a family to accomplish something worthwhile and lasting in the lives of others.

One of the young women on staff at the home had a friend with an unusual ministry in Guatemala City. She asked our teenagers if they would like to go along with her to visit her friend. They thought it sounded like a fun trip. Jana told us later how surprised she was when Sue drove them to the city trash dump. Jana said that as they neared the dump, she could see vultures circling overhead and picking around in the trash. As they came closer she saw other animals moving around in the garbage. She was shocked when she realized that it was not just dogs and vultures picking through the trash, but people—men, women and children. This made a powerful impression on her.

Kari, Sue's friend, runs a school for the children who live in the dump. She explained to our teenagers how God gave her a vision for the school. She had started with a small group of kids, but by that time nearly a hundred kids were coming to the school each day. There the children receive two meals a day and get regular baths and showers. Kari also finds volunteer professionals to come to the school to do medical and dental work for the children. Kari told the kids stories of how garbage trucks will sometimes back in and dump trash on small children without knowing it. The children suffocate and die under the pile of rubbish, and nobody ever sees them again. She explained how families in the dump make money by recycling trash, and she talked about the terrible problems that come from malnutrition and sniffing glue. This experience was powerful and life-changing for our boys and Jana. It was so memorable to Jana that she wrote about it in her college entrance essay as her most significant experience in life.

On other trips to Guatemala I have tried to take at least one of our children with me. These one-on-one times together, doing significant hands-on ministry, working out problems together and supporting one another, have been great learning experiences and deep bonding times. As a result our children have always enjoyed and been more excited about mission trips to Mexico to build houses for the poor than they have about ski trips or youth camps.

Some of your family times together should focus on loving others and making a difference in the world. Teaching each other by example how to reach out *beyond* ourselves and become a blessing to others is the most powerful way for our families to learn together what God's love is really all about.

Questions for Discussion

1. Discuss together the statement made on page 173, "Our primary goal as Christian parents will always be to find as many ways as we can—verbally and nonverbally—to let each child know: *there is nothing you can ever do to make me love you more; there*

is nothing you could ever do to make me love you less."

2. Why is it hard for us to let our children develop naturally according to their individual gifts and interests? Why do we feel the need to pressure our children and impose an agenda for their lives? What is the appropriate balance in parenting that leads to a posture of gentle guidance rather than manipulation?

3. Do you agree that "quantity time" with kids and with spouse is required to produce the real "quality times"? How can you work toward finding larger blocks of time to spend with your family?

4. Describe one event or experience your family shared that was especially fun for everyone. What made it so enjoyable? Is it something other families could plan to do?

5. Why do you think saying "I love you" through a touch or a hug can be so powerful for both kids and adults? Discuss what level of physical affection you consider to be healthy in a family and what boundaries may need to be created at different stages of a child's growth. If touching is not natural in your family, what other ways have you developed to show warmth and affection?

6. When was the last time you asked for forgiveness from one of your children? Are you able to do this easily?

7. Does your family have a contagious atmosphere of verbally affirming one another? Why does it seem so much easier to spot and speak out about the negative than to see and encourage the positive in one another? What steps can your family take toward building one another up more consistently?

8. What are you doing to prepare your children to accept Christ as their personal Savior and Lord?

9. How are you as a family reaching out in love to those outside of your family circle?

12
Tempted
to Forget
the Discipline

•

Judie and I were absolutely lost as parents with our first child, Jana. She was a beautiful little girl whom we nearly ruined through poor, indecisive parenting. As a toddler, she would not play alone. If we left her and walked out of the room, even for a moment, she would wail at the top of her lungs and throw herself on the floor in a temper tantrum. If she was in her playpen and we walked away, she would scream bloody murder until she got us to come back. She would not sleep through the night—she would wake up several times each night during her first two years, crying and yelling until we gave in. We were at a loss to know what to do.

Fortunately we had Christian friends who cared enough about us to take us aside and give us counsel. We protested a bit at first. As parents we don't want to admit that we might be the reason for our child's bad behavior. We tried telling these older and wiser Christian parents that we had just been given a bad kid, stubborn and strong-willed. But they weren't buying the line. Little by little we began learning that we were making significant mistakes that contributed to Jana's problem behavior.

The most important thing we learned was that we were unwittingly positively reinforcing Jana's negative behaviors. Basically, we were teaching and training into her the worst behaviors by rewarding her screaming and tantrums and giving in to her demands. And anytime you positively reinforce a behavior in your kids you can expect that behavior to grow in intensity and to be repeated. This is what was happening with Jana. When she cried at night, we always went in to check on her. We gave her special attention. We would rock or walk her back to sleep, or give her a drink and something to eat. If she screamed when we left the room, we would go back and get her and bring her along with us. It seemed innocent enough at the beginning. But as things got worse, it was not much fun being a parent to this out-of-control child.

If this kind of parenting problem continues long enough, it produces demanding and selfish children who will never quit whining or screaming until they get their way. Children rule in these families. There is almost no limit to what confused parents will do as they allow themselves to be driven by their kids. Judie and I know from experience what a terrible trap this can be and how easy it is to fall into it.

We have friends who are just beginning to learn some of these tough lessons with their young children. They began to wonder whether they had let things get out of control when they found themselves having to take their eighteen-month-old out for an hour-long "nighty-night ride" every evening in order to get the child to go to sleep. If he woke up on the way back into the house, they would have to do it all over again. Excessive parental responses like these are always a clue that somewhere early on the child gained control of the household.

But don't be too discouraged if you are struggling now to regain proper parental authority. Things can always be turned around. We can all learn to give consistent discipline to our children and maintain a healthy family environment that will be good for the kids and better for us as parents. Our goal in learning to discipline is to get to the place where the kids behave well enough that we can thoroughly enjoy them, whether we are at home, out shopping, having dinner in a restaurant or visiting another family. You should be able to do with your children all the things you always enjoyed doing as a couple before having children.

Family researchers Jack and Judith Balswick believe the strongest and most effective parents learn how to lovingly manage their homes by creating an environment in which there is a good balance of affirmation and control. Children need good boundaries for their behavior. Discipline is the key to directing a child's energy toward productive rather than destructive behaviors.

The Balswicks suggest that there are four possible parenting styles that grow out of combinations of high and low support along with high and low control. Figure 2 diagrams these four styles.

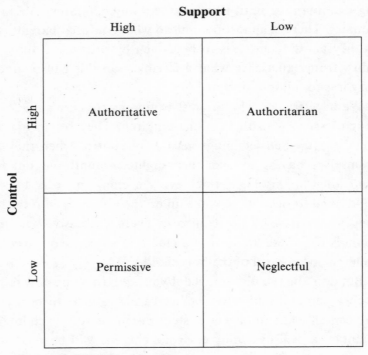

Figure 2. Parenting styles

Parents who give little support and little control are called *neglectful*. Basically, the children in these families do not experience healthy parental involvement in their lives, either through affirmation or through control. These children have a difficult time later on learning to discipline themselves so that they will be productive in life. They often struggle with self-esteem problems and actually long for authority and direction in their lives. Recent studies show that most recruits to cults come from neglectful homes.[1] It is suggested that these people have a desperate need to bond with a strong authoritarian figure. Children from neglectful families will struggle with identity and self-esteem, establishing consistent personal values and determining a life direction. They have a hard time making and keeping commitments, which leads to an inability to maintain relationships over the long term.

Authoritarian parents are controlling but do not express affirmation or support. Children in these homes will often be obedient, but there is no intimacy between the child and the authoritarian parent. Often one parent will be strongly authoritarian while the other is relational and supportive. This can bring some emotional health and stability into the family. But children who have lived under a dominant and unloving parent will encounter various crises in relationships, self-identity and values once they leave home. It is difficult to know who you really are if you have not been affirmed as a young person. It is hard to know what you really believe if all of your behavior has simply been a fearful response to a powerful, overriding authority figure.

Parents who affirm and support their children but do not discipline well would be considered *permissive* parents. I grew up in a permissive home. My father had been abused as a child. He was admirable in his ability to rise above the patterns of his upbringing. When we needed decisive discipline, however, my dad was not able to do it. My mom and my dad both affirmed us, and we all felt loved. But every one of the children in our family has struggled to some degree with self-discipline. Learning how to manage my life and how to be self-disciplined has been a constant uphill battle for me. The other aspect of our family upbringing that is common in permissive families was adolescent rebellion that leads to counterculture attitudes. Both rebellion against authority and the desire and need for stronger authority are present in varying degrees in children who come from permissive homes.

The Balswicks say the following about what they call an *authoritative* style of parenting:

> It has been well documented that socially competent children are products of homes in which the parenting style is authoritative. Social competence results when parents attend to their children's self-esteem, academic achievement, cognitive development, creativity, moral behavior, and instrumental abilities. Children thrive in such an environment of high support and high control.[2]

Children are more likely to exhibit competence and a healthy self-concept if they grow up in homes where reasonable limits are set and loving affirmation is given. In a University of Minnesota study it was also shown that children from authoritative homes were more likely to follow the religious heritage of their parents and were better "spiritually adjusted." These children on the whole worked better with all authority figures and therefore tended to do better in school, sports and other settings where adapting to proper authority led to success. Authoritative families had the fewest cases of counterculture rebellion.[3]

Learning to Set Limits

Judie and I learned from more experienced parents how to be decisive when it was needed. Love does have to be tough sometimes. We also grew wiser and more discerning in recognizing the many types of manipulation children cleverly use to control us as parents. Unacceptable behavior needs to receive immediate and appropriate consequences from parents. Disobedient children should not be told, "You wait until your dad gets home," nor should they be given twelve warnings before any action is taken. Your children learn quickly how many warnings each parent will give before acting. And they will take you to the limit. They also learn that they can escape punishment if they quickly apologize when discipline finally looks imminent (after the twelfth "If you don't stop that, you're going to get a spanking!"). Both parents need to act in a timely fashion when discipline is required. If the family rules and consequences are well understood, one warning—even as subtle as a raised eyebrow—should be enough.

Judie and I have observed families that we would describe as authoritative in style. Their firm discipline administered in love produced the sweetest children. In Christian families where kids were affirmed often, and yet love was also tough when it needed to be, the children displayed the kind of character and lovely qualities we hoped for in our own kids.

We saw that children from these families were on the whole more loving and gentle than kids growing up in secular homes. They were kind to animals and to smaller children. These were the boys and girls who unselfishly reached out to unpopular kids on the block and at school, being friends to these kids when no one else would. We saw that these were families in which brothers and sisters often expressed an uncommon love and appreciation for each other. They took care of and watched over the younger kids in the family, and astonishingly, they even seemed on the whole to take more pleasure in giving and sharing than in having everything for themselves.

We came to believe that these things could be possible for our kids, and that this type of behavior should be typical of children like ours who grew up in Christian families. If you are struggling in this area, there are many resources available through good Christian organizations like Focus on the Family. Stay close to families who are a few steps ahead of you in their level of parenting. Choose families that seem to you to be doing an excellent job in parenting because you can see the fruit of the Spirit in their children. Learn everything you can from them. Don't be embarrassed to ask for help.

Jana turned out to be a lovely young person once we stopped training her to be a hyperactive screamer with our faulty parenting habits. We quit giving in to her negative behaviors and started positively reinforcing her better behavior. In a very short time, she became a completely different person.

I will never forget the night we finally decided to be resolute in ignoring her crying when she woke up at 2:00 a.m. She screamed so loudly that we had to go outside and pray that we could outlast her. There was nothing wrong with her. She wasn't sick, wet or hungry. We had just trained her to expect us to come in whenever she cried. We had to break this pattern. We had to begin the difficult job of untraining that undesirable behavior. That first night she cried for over half an hour. Then she slept the rest of the night. The second night she woke up crying. We ignored it. She went back to sleep in less than five minutes. After that, Jana slept through the night.

When we adopted the twins, and then had Gabe shortly thereafter, we had four children under five years of age. We had to have a naptime, bedtime and mealtime schedule that worked for us as a family. We found that encouraging good behavior and refusing to positively reinforce bad behavior helped us create a home environment that was for the most part pleasant for everyone.

When one of the toddler twins cried and whined in order to be picked up, we would say in the right tone, "Mommy and Daddy are not going to pick you up when you're acting like that." A little while later when he stopped fussing, one of us would hold him or play with him for a while. Our kids got more attention when they were good than when they were bad. We got better at training good behavior into our children and became wiser at analyzing behavior problems and how to deal with them.

Any recurring bad behavior in our children can usually be traced to some regular, positive reinforcement of the behavior by one or both of us as parents. We need to identify how we are encouraging bad behavior and break the pattern. Then we need to positively reinforce the desired behavior. This takes some work and good communication between Mom and Dad, but it is well worth it.

Raising Our Vision

I believe we have lost a vision for what our children can be. We should look to the Bible for the standards of attitude and behavior we hope to encourage in our kids. Too often we accept a lower standard of behavior because it's accepted in the broader culture. But I believe we can have children who display character and caring. As parents we have to work diligently and pray diligently that God will help us learn how to cooperate better with the work of the Holy Spirit to encourage the maturing of our children toward biblical goals.

The following is a list of biblically based attitudes and behaviors we would hope to see developing in children of Christian families:

1. Christian children should respect and respond to proper authority. This is really the central issue in Christianity: will we respond to proper authority or will we rebel? Children need to be responsive to proper authority. If we fail to teach this, we fail to prepare our children for a meaningful personal relationship with the Lord Christ.

2. Children growing up in Christian homes should display an increasing interest in the things of God, including God in their thoughts, talk and play.

3. Maturing Christian children should also be developing a giving attitude that recognizes the importance of unselfish sharing.

4. Learning how and when to say "I'm sorry" is a difficult but essential biblical life principle. Learning to ask forgiveness of God and others and to grant forgiveness is an essential life skill for Christian kids.

5. Christian children should be growing in their ability to em-

pathize and sympathize with others, developing the skills needed to encourage rather than criticize.

6. As a general principle, Christian children should show an increasing willingness to act in accordance with their developing conscience under parenting that is guided by the values inherent in biblical Christianity.

7. Our children should demonstrate a developing confidence and self-esteem that is rooted in their internalized knowledge that they are loved unconditionally by Christ.

8. If we are successful in helping our children understand and respond to the good news of the gospel, we also ought to see in them a growing dependence on Jesus as Savior and Lord, a greater obedience to God's Word and a maturing prayer life. It is not the acceptance of a value system that we are after with our kids, but a living relationship with the living Christ.

Learning to Let Go

No matter how good a job we do in parenting, we will still experience many problems and setbacks. We are sinful people. We will make many mistakes. Judie and I are at the point now where the largest portion of our parenting is behind us. We will learn how well our children have adopted the values we have hoped would be formed in them only as we watch them step out into the world on their own, live and grow independently, marry, have children and parent their own kids.

All four of our children are now out of the home and living on their own. At this stage we begin moving beyond discipline to dialogue with our adult children. Some discipline is still required. Your daughter will need to learn how to handle her personal finances. You will have to decide what you will help with and what she has to cover on her own, and what consequences she can expect if she fails to live up to her side of the bargain. Your son will need to learn how to maintain his car. If he does not keep oil in his car and he blows the engine, he may have to walk, bike or take the bus until he can save enough money to buy something else or get the engine fixed. At this stage, natural consequences are a very good teacher. This is real life: if you don't take care of things, there is a price to pay.

Most of what Judie and I find ourselves doing now is talking with our children about the choices they are making. We may help them decide life directions or share ideas about an upcoming job interview, but mostly when they ask us for help and advice. Parenting can be very tough at this stage because kids make so many decisions with which we disagree. We are thankful for good communication patterns in our family. Our adult children still call to talk to us about their decisions, even about those decisions that are contrary to our values and go against what we have taught in our home. At those times Judie and I sometimes joke together about wishing the kids wouldn't call—that we'd rather not know. But this is not really true.

It is unrealistic to think that four children leaving home and trying their wings on their own for the first time are going to do everything we would want them to without making mistakes. Judie gave a Mother's Day talk at the church recently and said this stage, more than any other, requires our unconditional love as parents. The kids are out on their own; we are no longer in control. They will often choose to go their own way. Will we still love them? Will we pray for them when they ask for prayer, even though they're making a choice with which we disagree?

We work hard at keeping the relationships intact, at expressing our love even when we are hurt and disappointed at one of our children's choices. Our kids realize that their choices do sometimes change what we can or cannot support financially and in other ways. That's how we relate honestly and lovingly with them as adult friends. We have to make these tough choices. It does not change the fact that we love them. And they love us.

So far we have been fortunate, maintaining good relationships and good patterns of communication with our adult children. We hope it continues. But we realize there are no guarantees in parenting, even for those who do an excellent job of parenting. We have shared in the pain of many parents who we believe have done a much better job at parenting than we have, but who have watched one or more of their kids slip away from them. There is no deeper pain than losing one of your children. It hurts when a child turns away, closes the door, rejects the family and rejects God. It has helped us at times to remember that God himself— the perfect parent—created two perfect children and placed them in a perfect environment, and yet they chose to rebel against him.

Being a good parent does not automatically produce children who live in love and faithfulness. We can't make our children's decisions for them, and we're not their saviors. Only Jesus can be your child's Savior. God is ultimately responsible for our children. They belong to him. They always have. We have to do the best job we can, but ultimately they are in God's hands.

In this respect, probably the most productive thing we can do as parents is to continue to pray for our children daily. Trust your sons and daughters to the loving hands of God. Ask God for wisdom to see his vision for each of your children's lives, and hold this vision up in prayer. Ask him daily for the energy and courage it takes to be a good and faithful parent in these tough times.

Questions for Discussion

1. Of the four parenting styles listed, which would you identify as closest to the parenting style in your home as you were growing up? How would you characterize the style in your family today?

2. As husband and wife, do your parenting styles differ? How? Do they complement one another, making for a good balance? Or do you think your differences may be counterproductive? What changes would you like to see in your parenting styles?

3. What kinds of situations with your children do you find the most difficult to manage? Discuss some ideas in this chapter that strike you as especially helpful and practical. What can you im-

mediately put to use in your parenting?

4. The author believes that many parents today have lost their vision for what their children can be and what kind of character can be built in their kids through good parenting. Do you agree or disagree? Why?

5. What are the most significant changes parents face when their children grow through the adolescent stage and begin life on their own? Do parents still have to parent as a child grows into mature adulthood? Discuss strategies for parenting adult children.

13
Tempted to
Give Up
on God

•

Gary and Joan had written us and other friends asking
for our prayers. They knew ahead of time that their baby would
be born with a heart defect. We love Gary and Joan. We prayed
earnestly for little Nathan. Then we received this announcement
in the mail from our friends.

Nathan James LeTourneau
"Gift of God"
July 1, 1994—July 9, 1994

Nathan was born Friday evening, July 1st. We had the unan-
ticipated pleasure of being able to hold him for about ten minutes in the delivery room before he was transferred to the Neo-
natal Intensive Care Unit. He was so beautifully formed that it
was hard to believe that anything was wrong with him.

His open heart surgery was performed on Tuesday, July 5th.
The operation did not go as well as we hoped. His heart was
unable to beat as he was taken off the heart/lung machine, and
we thought we were going to lose him then. The doctors were
able to get his heart beating, but he remained in extremely

critical condition in the days following surgery. On Friday afternoon he took a downward turn, and on Saturday morning he died in Gary's arms with Joan at his side.

Thank you for your prayers and concern.

> *He gathers the lambs in his arms*
> *and carries them close to his heart.*
> *Isaiah 40:11*

On the inside cover was the familiar passage from Psalm 139, "For you created my inmost being; you knit me together in my mother's womb. . . . All the days ordained for me were written in your book before one of them came to be" (vv. 13, 16).

Gary is a pastor in Minnesota. He and Joan have another child, a little two-year-old daughter named Hannah. She is a miracle baby they had after thinking they were not going to be able to have children. Gary told me little Hannah has lately been praying that God would make the owee go away in Mommy's eyes.

I talked with Gary shortly after receiving the news of Nathan's death. He was so sad, hurting so deeply. He told me he still thought he wanted to be a pastor.

When as Christians we are hit with this kind of devastating pain, we are affected on two levels. There is the raw pain of the loss itself—the hurt, the grief, the open wound. But our pain is also tangled up with questions about where God is in the midst of our struggle.

We believe that he loves us. That's what the Bible teaches. But then we're knocked for a loop with something in life that makes us wonder, "God, where are you? Why have you turned away? Why are you silent? Don't you hear me? Don't you care?" The deeper agony for all of us might be the fear we experience, the fear that comes when we wonder if there really is someone out there who hears and cares.

During the first eight years of our married life, Judie and I were childless. Some of you know what this is like. There is the painful recurring monthly cycle—the praying and hoping that perhaps some new idea from the doctor or a recent magazine article will finally help. You try to maintain a positive attitude, believing that this will finally be the time, that this month there will be a good sign, only to have your hopes dashed at the end of the cycle. Then you try to prepare yourself to start the painful process over again.

I remember vividly those questions in my mind: "God, where are you? Don't you hear us? Why are you silent?" For us the pain was always deepened by the insensitive comments from relatives and acquaintances: "Don't you think it's about time the two of you started your family? Is there something wrong with you?"

The other thing that always hurt us was hearing couples gripe and complain about their kids, gesturing toward them and saying, "This is our third little mistake, and over there is Jesse, our fourth mistake." These couples seemed only to have to breathe on each other to get pregnant. We were always running into people who did not really want and appreciate the kids they had when we desperately wanted children and could not even have one.

After eight years we decided to adopt. We adopted a biracial baby. We had two-month-old Jana in our home after waiting only a year. Judie and I both remember vividly that little one-by-two-inch picture of our new little girl that the social worker showed us the day she called us in to tell us they had a baby for us.

Were we excited? Judie went right home and wrote this:

As we prepare to receive you
We feel a deep stirring excitement
  Of Love
    Of warmth
      Of Parenthood.
We see your smile in our smile,
Hear your laughter in our laughter,
Feel your love in our love, dear little girl.

Who are you?
You are us: our joy, our love, our child.
You are the fulfillment of dreams,
    The pink dawn of new days,
    The glitter of stars on forever warm nights.
You are our daughter.

We thank our sweet God for the blessing of you
and dedicate you to him for safekeeping.

Welcome, Jana Lee.

What a blessed day! This was a wonderful time for us. God seemed so close. So real. He was there. He had heard our pleas and remembered us.

Just two years later, Judie got pregnant for the first time. Talk about sky-high! It had never happened in ten years of marriage. God continued to bless us. I took my first teaching job in Rochester, Minnesota, and we settled into a new town and a new church with our little family and our second child on the way.

Then in the fourth month, Judie started spotting. When she called the doctor, he said not to worry. She went to see him the next day. I remember how crushed and numbed we both were by the news Judie shared with me when she got home. We were so stunned we could hardly cry at first. Our baby was dead. A rare tumor that grows only in a fertile womb had taken over the space in that small sanctuary and killed our child.

I remember everything about the day Judie went in for surgery. I can still feel the damp chill of the Midwest winter on my cheeks. I can still see the gray, overcast sky and picture the Olmsted Community Hospital in Rochester, the lawn, the dirt on the snow, the dead leaves along the drive. I remember the waiting room, where I sat alone during the operation.

"God. How could you do this? We prayed for years that you

would bless us in this way. You answered our prayers, we thought. Then you took this child away. Why even let Judie get pregnant if you knew it was going to turn out this way?"

I don't think I've ever felt more alone. We were so new in the community that most of the members in our little church didn't even know that Judie was pregnant. Most never knew we lost this baby. There was nothing we could do but cling to each other, and we did cling to God.

Judie was really strong at first. When the doctor confirmed his diagnosis and visited her in her room, he sat on the edge of her bed with tears in his eyes and said, "Why you? This is the first time I have ever seen this tumor in one of my patients in twenty-five years of practice. It is that rare. Why you?"

Judie just said, "Why not me?"

But later, after the surgery, as the weeks went on, she got more angry at God. We both did. "God, why didn't you leave well enough alone? We had Jana. We were perfectly happy. Why allow this pregnancy and then cut it short?"

We will never know why we lost the child from that first pregnancy. That was one of the darkest times of our lives. We had anger that we had to work through. There was the grieving, the loss, the hurt and disappointment that come when the thing you desire most in life is torn away from you in ugliness and pain. But it was that event that led us to adopt again, two years later. This time it was twins—Jason and Josh. Then the extraordinary, unexpected event. Judie became pregnant again, immediately following the adoption. Now we were wondering about God's timing. What a sense of humor our God has: he waits until we adopt twins and then blesses us with a pregnancy! We were carrying three babies around everywhere we went.

It is not hard to figure out why Judie and I love our kids so much. They did not come to us without struggle. We can never see our children as anything but a great blessing from God, a wonderful gift. It is not hard for us to praise God now that our quiver is full, to use a biblical expression. It is not difficult to feel the closeness and presence of God when you are blessed.

This is not everyone's experience. If the blessing doesn't come, what do we do then? What about the couple who are childless and the child does not come? When there is an irretrievable loss in your life, how do you go on? Why is it that God will intervene in one case and apparently do nothing in another?

I remember being at a church conference a couple of years ago when a woman got up and shared a story about how her small child was miraculously saved from drowning. I don't remember all the details, but I believe the woman was working in the back yard, quite a distance from the house, when she heard the telephone ring. She said she would normally have let the answering machine take the call, but she felt an inner urging to answer the phone. And after a couple of rings she ran back toward the house to get it. When she neared the pool in the back yard, she saw that her baby had fallen in and was drowning. She came just in time to pull him out and save his life.

Everyone was moved by the story. It made you feel so good. There was cheering and clapping in the auditorium.

After things quieted down, another woman came forward to share. She told the group with much grief in her voice and tears in her eyes that her little child had drowned in the family's swimming pool. Her son had died. No telephone had rung for her. You could have heard a pin drop in that crowd.

I do not pretend to have an answer to this difficult problem of pain. But I have learned some things about God by experiencing personal struggle and helping and observing others who go through painful experiences. I'll tell one more story of a tragic and painful experience some friends of ours faced recently. Then I think I can say some things about where God is in the midst of these devastating times.

Late one summer night a few years ago, twenty-one-year-old Kirsten Davis was driving on a small Georgia highway on her way to visit a friend. She had just graduated from Berry College. Her parents, Barb and Dave, who are good friends of ours from Boulder, Colorado, had told us how much she loved the school, how much she was loved there, how well things were going for Kirsten and what a beautiful time of life this was for her.

As she drove alone down Highway 297 on a dark, drizzly night, just eighty feet from the bridge over Pendleton Creek, a car pulled up alongside her Subaru station wagon. Someone stuck a shotgun out the passenger side window and pulled the trigger. Police reports said the barrel of the gun must have been only eighteen inches from the side of Kirsten's face when the shot was fired, striking her in the jaw and neck. She was killed instantly. Her car veered across the road, rolled over and landed upside down in the ditch. The investigation continues to this day with no substantial clues as to who murdered Kirsten Davis, a pleasant college kid who had just graduated and was stepping onto the threshold of the rest of her life.

Some time ago when I was back in Boulder for a couple of days, I called Dave and Barb. I worried about what I would say. What do you say? Everything we've ever heard as explanations for difficult things we experience sound so hollow in the face of a loss like this: "Don't waste your pain. God is teaching you something." Or "Don't worry, 1 Corinthians 10:13 promises he will not test you beyond what you can bear." Or "This is an opportunity for you to grow in your faith. Consider it a joy when you face trials of many kinds, because the trial will produce perseverance and character." Or "Remember, all things work together for good for those who love the Lord."

When I tried to get together with Dave and Barb it didn't work out. I called their home, but Barb told me they had a dozen students from Berry College staying with them for the night. The students were on a ski trip to Colorado and had called ahead to ask if they could stay with the Davises. She explained what had been going on all evening. The kids came by so they could tell

Dave and Barb what Kirsten had meant to them, what kind of friend and person she was. Barb told me what a beautiful time it was for them to hear all these kids telling their personal stories about Kirsten—her caring, her sense of humor, her positive involvement in the lives of others.

Barb had earlier told me about the caring expressed by so many others that helped them through this tough time. She talked about the investigation, how personally the Georgia Bureau of Investigation officers took Kirsten's case. Glynn Meeks, special agent in charge of the thirteen-county region where Kirsten was killed, keeps her picture on the front of his file cabinet where he can see her every day. Kirsten had been working to raise money to buy a flagpole for Win Shape Center at Berry College when she died. A hundred students gathered to dedicate the new pole in her name. A group of Kirsten's closest friends gathered and planted a pink dogwood tree at Swan Lake on the campus. The memorial at the base of the tree reads, "As this tree grows and lives, so does the memory of our dear friend, Kirsten Davis." The school meant so much to Kirsten that her mom and dad had her buried on a spot overlooking the campus rather than taking her back to Colorado.

One thing I know. In the face of Kirsten's tragic and meaningless death, the moment I ask, "Where were you, God? Why were you silent? Why didn't you intervene?" I can't help but get a vivid picture in my mind of those college kids sitting at the Davises', sharing with Barb and Dave individual stories of their deep love for a friend. When I talked with Gary LeTourneau a short time after Nathan's death, he too had story after story about the outpouring of love and care from their congregation, blessings of God poured out through the people in their church.

The reality and power of such demonstrations of deep love and sensitive caring change my perspective. Now other questions enter my mind. Instead of all the analytical doubts that can flood in concerning the problem of pain, I start wondering instead things like *Where does this kind of love come from? Why do people care?*

Now, instead of dwelling on the mystery of why God does not intervene at times, I am awed instead by the fact that there is love in the world at all. I have become convinced that if there was no God of love, no caring, personal, intimately involved God whose character is the controlling influence in this otherwise dark world, we would *all* be shotgun murderers.

Things That Seem to Make Sense

When I do not have an answer from God for why I have to experience times of deep pain, there are at least a couple of things that help me in the midst of my struggle. First, I am comforted to know that, like me, Jesus suffered in the flesh. And because he has experienced every kind of human pain and sorrow, he empathizes with my pain. Hebrews 2:18 says, "For since he himself has now been through suffering and temptation, he knows what it is like when we suffer and are tempted, and he is wonderfully able to help us" (LB). Because of Jesus and what he went through, I know that God understands my suffering. We never go through anything in our lives that God has not already endured himself. When I turn to God and cry out to him in my suffering, I know he hears me as one who has suffered, who shares in my pain, who has hurt in the same way I hurt.

God may not save me from pain or struggle in this life, but he is there. And he knows what it is like. He heard the cries of his own Son in the Garden of Gethsemane. He heard the cries of his Son from the cross. And he hears our cries today.

The death of Jesus stands as the most powerful statement ever about the paradox of pain and the will of God. Look at the cross. When God seemed to be the farthest away, he could not have been closer. Jesus cried out, "My God, my God, why have you forsaken me?" (Mt 27:46). The Lord of life was expressing heartfelt abandonment. Yet when God seems dead or aloof, it turns out that he is most truly alive and intimately involved. There at the cross he was accomplishing his most loving work—the salvation of all who

[210]

believe. God appears at times to be silent, but it is often during those times that he is the most active in our lives. We come to know this is true if we can turn toward God in faith in the midst of our suffering.

Second, I believe God loves us even more than we can possibly know, more than we can even love ourselves or those closest to us. C. S. Lewis gives us a vivid picture of this concept in one of the volumes in the Chronicles of Narnia. In these children's books Lewis has made a lion named Aslan the Christ-figure. In *The Magician's Nephew,* a young boy named Digory is responsible for bringing a wicked witch into the new world that Aslan has just created. Near the end he has to face Aslan for it. He is very frightened, for he knows the wrong he has done. Digory is also terribly worried about his mother, who is ill and dying. This is how Lewis portrays Christ in the dialogue between Digory and Aslan:

"Son of Adam," said Aslan. "Are you ready to undo the wrong that you have done to my sweet country of Narnia on the very day of its birth?"

"Well, I don't see what I can do," said Digory. "You see, the Queen ran away and—"

"I asked, are you ready," said the Lion.

"Yes," said Digory. He had had for a second some wild idea of saying, "I'll try to help you if you'll promise to help about my Mother," but he realized in time that the Lion was not at all the sort of person one could try to make bargains with. But when he had said "Yes," he thought of his Mother, and he thought of the great hopes he had had, and how they were all dying away, and a lump came in his throat and tears in his eyes, and he blurted out:

"But please, please—won't you—can't you give me something that will cure Mother?" Up till then he had been looking at the Lion's great front feet and the huge claws on them; now, in his despair, he looked up at its face. What he saw surprised him as much as anything in his whole life. For the tawny face was bent down near his own and (wonder of wonders) great shining tears stood in the Lion's eyes. They were such big, bright tears compared with Digory's own that for a moment he felt as if the Lion must really be sorrier about his Mother than he was himself.

"My son, my son," said Aslan. "I know. Grief is great. Only you and I in this land know that yet. Let us be good to one another."[1]

When I hurt so badly I don't know what to do, this picture often comes into my mind. I see the powerful Lion of Judah, not his claws, but the great shiny tears in his eyes—tears of grief and pain. He enters into my pain because he loves me. And he loves those I love more than I can love them myself.

God Comforts Us So We Can Be a Comfort to Others

The third thing I have experienced and observed about our suffering is that God will minister love and grace to others through us if we have suffered. As he has comforted us, we will be able to comfort others. We can be assured that in God's economy, nothing significant that happens to us is ever wasted. The apostle Paul writes, "Praise be to the God and Father of our Lord Jesus Christ, the Father of compassion and the God of all comfort, who comforts us in all our troubles, so that we can comfort those in any trouble with the comfort we ourselves have received from God. For just as the sufferings of Christ flow over into our lives, so also through Christ our comfort overflows" (2 Cor 1:3-5).

I have never seen this Scripture more truly expressed in life than through the lives of Joe and Mary Lou Bayly. In the years before his death, Joe was a friend and mentor to me. He has been like a father to me in the faith. He and Mary Lou have taught me how to live through suffering, and how God will powerfully use those who have suffered.

There is probably nothing more painful in life than losing one of your children. Joe and Mary Lou lost three of their children on three separate occasions in a period of six years. One son died during a complex operation shortly after birth. Another son, Danny, died of leukemia at the age of four. A third son died from complications after a tobogganing accident.

I remember Joe and Mary Lou telling how Danny, their four-year-old, died. The cancer had gone into remission once. Then it got worse again. Joe said Danny woke up at home one morning bleeding. The pediatrician came to their home and said that Danny could be transferred to Children's Hospital for a massive blood transfusion, which might prolong his life for a week or two. Or he could stay there and die at home. Joe and Mary Lou decided that they wanted to have Danny with them at home.

Joe described Danny to me in this way. He said he was one of those little boys who from the earliest days have a hunger and love for God and the things of God. When some missionary friends of the Baylys were killed by the Auca Indians in South America, and Danny heard about it, he decided he wanted to be a missionary. Later, when Danny became severely ill, he decided he wanted to become a medical missionary. Near the end, Joe said, Danny was attended by a wonderful woman hematologist whom he grew to love. He changed his mind again. He decided he wanted to be a *woman* medical missionary.

The morning of the day Danny died was a miserable morning for all of them. Danny was suffering extreme pain from the cancer, and he did not want to leave Joe and Mary Lou and go to heaven. He would ask them repeatedly, "Will you go with me?" They would say, "No. We can't come now. But we will come later." Danny would say, "Then I don't want to go."

Joe said it was a terribly painful time for them as parents. Danny had such sorrow, anguish and suffering for a four-year-old little boy. But they knew in faith that at the moment of death, this lovely, unhappy little boy would be completely delivered from all the pain and sorrow he was going through.

Mary Lou said Danny turned toward her and asked, "How will I go to heaven?"

[213]

She said, "How would you like to go?"

He said, "I want Jesus to carry me."

"Then that's the way you will go," Mary Lou said. A moment later, he was gone.

Joe said that many questions remained unanswered, but at the same time they had no doubt of God's love. Three children dead within a six-year period. But they were sure of God's love. After all, hadn't God himself lost his only Son in pain and anguish? Joe told me, "We have never been more sure of God's love than we have been as we turned away from a fresh grave."

The day after Danny's funeral, Joe went to Children's Hospital to say thank you to the many doctors and nurses who had been so helpful to them and to Danny throughout his illness. While there he happened to meet a woman whose own son was struggling with leukemia. She talked with Joe about the difficult process of testing the bone marrow and then waiting for hours for the results, hoping against hope that the cancer might go into remission.

Joe said she talked about the test. "It's hard," she said. "I die every time I do it, and now he's starting to complain about it."

In his gentle way Joe said, "Isn't it good to know even when it appears there is no hope medically, that after this life and in the life to come, your child will be completely delivered from all the pain, the fear and the suffering?"

She said, "If only I could believe that. But when I cover my little boy over with dirt, I'll just have to forget I ever had a little boy."

Joe said, "I'm glad I don't feel that way."

"Why?" she said.

"Because we covered our little boy over with dirt yesterday afternoon."

After a long pause the woman spoke again. "You look like a rational person. How can you really believe that there is anything more for your little boy or for you after this life than there is for a dog or some other animal?"

Joe said, "For one reason only. One man died, never to die again." And as simply as possible he told her about Jesus' birth, life, death and resurrection from the dead, which gives every believer the power of hope over death.

One time Joe came to speak at a men's retreat for our church. That year a man who had just lost his five-year-old daughter came to the retreat. His daughter had stepped off her school bus to go to her kindergarten class. The driver didn't see her walk in front of the bus and he drove over her, killing her instantly.

This broken father asked Joe if he could ride back with us in the van from Colorado Springs to the Denver airport. As tired as Joe was, he quickly made the man feel comfortable and invited him to share the back seat of the van. I have never in my life been exposed to a more beautiful conversation. I sat quietly, listening and learning, as Joe talked with this hurting father. Joe's ability to empathize with the deepest feelings of this other man was extraordinary. He asked all the right questions that allowed this young man to pour out his grief, his anger, his doubts about God in the midst of his suffering. Joe also knew the areas of the young couple's marriage that would need attention because of what they were going through. His ability to love this father concretely, to join in his suffering and to direct him to the help he would need to put his life and marriage back together again was powerfully Spirit-led. It was one of the greatest privileges I've had as a Christian to witness God's healing power at work through one of his faithful servants who had suffered greatly but did not turn away from God in his pain.

I know that any suffering I experience here will allow me to bring comfort and love to others in the midst of their suffering. God will use your pain in the lives of others, if you offer it to him as a sacrifice of your love. In this way our pain and loss is redeemed by God in this world. And we can trust that all of our earthly pain will one day pale in comparison to the glory that will be ours.

The apostle Paul, who suffered as much as any man, had this perspective: "Our light and momentary troubles are achieving for us an eternal glory that far outweighs them all" (2 Cor 4:17). Paul's light and momentary troubles included beatings, shipwrecks, being stoned and left for dead, loneliness and heartache, concern for all the churches, and a thorn in the flesh. Paul continued to walk faithfully with his Lord because he knew that the difficult and painful experiences he faced in life would one day be swallowed up in the glory of God like a single hot coal swallowed up in the sea.

Remember the great shining tears of our Lord, who loves us more than we can love ourselves and loves those we love more completely than we could ever love them. We can trust a God like this.

Questions for Discussion

1. Have you ever been tempted to give up on God? If you feel comfortable doing so, describe the situation you faced and explain why it was so hard for you. Is the pain still there? Is this still a struggle for you? How are you and God getting through it?

2. The author believes a key to living effectively in painful times is to be able to turn toward God in our suffering. Is this your pattern? Do you turn toward God in difficult times? How has this helped you to get through a dark period? How has God responded to you as you have cried out to him for help?

3. Has God given you an ability to help and comfort others after you have been through painful times? Has this been meaningful to you?

4. How does it make you feel when you remember that Christ has also suffered deeply and empathizes with your pain? Can you picture the tears of Christ as he hurts with you during painful periods in your life?

5. The author says that our most painful experiences in life will "one day be swallowed up in the glory of God like a single hot coal

[216]

swallowed up in the sea." Does it help you to think on this image and hold this perspective in your mind? Discuss the meaning of this statement and of the 2 Corinthians 4:17 passage quoted at the end of the chapter.

Notes

Chapter 1: Tempted to Let Life's Rush Swallow Us Up

[1] Jack O. Balswick and Judith K. Balswick, *The Family: A Christian Perspective on the Contemporary Home* (Grand Rapids, Mich.: Baker Book House, 1989), p. 297.

[2] Dan Levin, "What's Up Doc?" *Sports Illustrated* 55 (October 19, 1981): 109.

[3] Mike Bellah, *Baby Boom Believers: Why We Think We Need It All and How to Survive When We Don't Get It* (Wheaton, Ill.: Tyndale House, 1988), p. 136.

[4] Diana Hales and Robert R. Hales, "Babes In Stressland," *American Health,* October 1989, p. 52.

[5] Ibid., p. 56.

[6] Sylvia Ann Hewlett, *When the Bough Breaks: The Cost of Neglecting Our Children* (New York: BasicBooks, 1991), pp. 106-7.

[7] Ibid., pp. 76-77.

[8] Ibid., pp. 74-78.

Chapter 2: Tempted to Be an Absentee Father

[1] Gary Smith, "As Time Runs Out," *Sports Illustrated* 78 (January 11, 1993): 18.

[2] Frank F. Furstenberg Jr. and Christine Winquist Nord, "Parenting Apart: Patterns of Childrearing After Marital Disruption," *Journal of Marriage and the Family* 47 (November 1985): 874.

[3] Leanne Payne, *Crisis in Masculinity* (Westchester, Ill.: Crossway Books, 1985), p. 14.

[4] Quoted from John W. Miller, *Biblical Faith and Fathering: Why We Call God "Father"* (New York: Paulist, 1989), p. 116.

[5] Quoted from Mary Stewart Van Leeuwen, *Gender and Grace: Love, Work and Parenting in a Changing World* (Downers Grove, Ill.: InterVarsity Press, 1990), p. 157.

[6] Ibid., p. 116.

[7] Ibid., pp. 117-18.

[8] Miller, *Biblical Faith and Fathering,* p. 69.

[9] In reading Leanne Payne, I have been impressed with the importance of healing memories through prayer, and especially of loving and forgiving our fathers as

a key to loving and accepting ourselves. The concepts expressed in these last few paragraphs are drawn from Payne's healing prayers, especially those in *Crisis in Masculinity.*

Chapter 3: Tempted to Wonder—Is Being a Mom Worth the Trouble?
[1]*The Boulder Camera,* February 13, 1983, p. 4A.
[2]George F. Gilder, *Sexual Suicide* (New York: Quadrangle, 1973), pp. 244-46.
[3]Harold M. Voth, "Women's Liberation: Cause and Consequence of Social Sickness," *New Oxford Review,* December 1980, pp. 8-12.
[4]Sylvia Ann Hewlett, *When the Bough Breaks: The Cost of Neglecting Our Children* (New York: BasicBooks, 1991), p. 54.
[5]Sylvia Ann Hewlett, "Running Hard Just to Keep Up," *Women: The Road Ahead,* special issue of *Time* 136, no. 19 (Fall 1990): 54.
[6]William J. Doherty, "Private Lives, Public Values," *Psychology Today,* May/June 1992, p. 35.

Chapter 4: Tempted to Miscommunicate
[1]I received this anonymous piece from my friend Paul, whose story I told in the previous chapter.
[2]John Powell, *Why Am I Afraid to Tell You Who I Am?* (Niles, Ill.: Argus Communications, 1972), pp. 43-85.
[3]David W. Augsburger, *Sustaining Love: Healing and Growth in the Passages of Marriage* (Ventura, Calif.: Regal, 1988), pp. 11-13.
[4]Bert Decker, *You've Got to Be Believed to Be Heard* (New York: St. Martin's, 1992), pp. 83-84.
[5]Ibid., pp. 48-49, 282-83.

Chapter 5: Tempted to Ignore the Differences Between Men and Women
[1]Gilbert Bilezikian, *Beyond Sex Roles: A Guide for the Study of Female Roles in the Bible* (Grand Rapids, Mich.: Baker Book House, 1985), pp. 55, 229, as quoted in Mary Stewart Van Leeuwen, *Gender and Grace: Love, Work and Parenting in a Changing World* (Downers Grove, Ill.: InterVarsity Press, 1990), p. 44.
[2]Deborah Tannen, *You Just Don't Understand: Women and Men in Conversation* (New York: Morrow, 1990). In this chapter I am indebted to Tannen for her insights, principles, research and observations.
[3]Ibid., p. 26.
[4]Ibid., p. 27.
[5]Ibid., pp. 49-50.

Chapter 6: Tempted to Neglect Speaking the Truth in Love
[1]Ray S. Anderson and Dennis B. Guernsey, *On Being Family: A Social Theol-*

ogy of the Family (Grand Rapids, Mich.: Eerdmans, 1985), p. 40.

[2]Walter Wangerin Jr., *As for Me and My House: Crafting Your Marriage to Last* (Nashville: Thomas Nelson, 1987), p. 195.

Chapter 7: Tempted to Lose Our Family Closeness
[1]Merton P. Strommen and A. Irene Strommen, *Five Cries of Parents* (San Francisco: Harper & Row, 1985), p. 72.

Chapter 8: Tempted to Misunderstand Family Leadership
[1]Those interested in a careful exegetical study of this passage may wish to refer to the work of Markus Barth, *Ephesians 4-6,* Anchor Bible Commentary (Garden City, N.Y.: Doubleday, 1981), pp. 607-50. Barth's translation attempts to capture as precisely as is possible in English the meaning of the original language. Though this leads to a less readable text than your favorite translation, Barth's insights into the language help us understand some of the more subtle emphases in Paul's writings on the marriage relationship.

[2]John Temple Bristow, *What Paul Really Said About Women: An Apostle's Liberating Views on Equality in Marriage, Leadership and Love* (San Francisco: HarperCollins, 1991), pp. 20, 32.

[3]Ibid., pp. 36-37.

[4]John Stott, as quoted in Lyman Coleman and Richard Peace, *Ephesians* (Littleton, Colo.: Serendipity House, 1986), p. 54.

[5]Tom L. Eisenman, *Temptations Men Face: Straightforward Talk on Power, Money, Affairs, Perfectionism, Insensitivity* (Downers Grove, Ill.: InterVarsity Press, 1990), pp. 120-21.

Chapter 9: Tempted to Blur Boundaries
[1]Henry Cloud and John Townsend, *Boundaries: When to Say Yes, When to Say No to Take Control of Your Life* (Grand Rapids, Mich.: Zondervan, 1992), p. 59.

[2]*San Ramon Valley Times,* July 8, 1991, p. 1.

[3]"Safety Tips on a Sensitive Subject: Child Sexual Abuse," Church Mutual Protection Series (Merrill, Wisc.: Church Mutual, 1986), p. 2.

[4]Maxine Hancock and Karen Burton Mains, *Child Sexual Abuse: A Hope for Healing* (Wheaton, Ill.: Harold Shaw, 1987), p. 12.

[5]Ibid., p. 141.

[6]Kathleen, *Healing from Sexual Abuse* (Downers Grove, Ill.: InterVarsity Press, 1991), p. 31.

[7]Cloud and Townsend, *Boundaries,* pp. 45-46.

[8]Ibid., p. 246.

[9]Ibid., p. 271.

Chapter 10: Tempted to Be a Couch Potato Family

[1]Pete Hamill, "Crack and the Box," *Esquire Magazine* 113 (May 1990): 63-65.

[2]Ibid., pp. 63-64.

[3]Quoted from Sylvia Ann Hewlett, *When the Bough Breaks: The Cost of Neglecting Our Children* (New York: BasicBooks, 1991), p. 94. See also Richard Zoglin, "Is TV Ruining Our Children?" *Time* 136 (October 15, 1990): 75-76.

[4]Hamill, "Crack and the Box," p. 64.

[5]"Would You Give Up TV for a Million Bucks?" *TV Guide,* October 10-16, 1992, pp. 10-17.

[6]Ibid., p. 11.

[7]Quentin J. Schultze, *Redeeming Television: How TV Changes Christians, How Christians Can Change TV* (Downers Grove, Ill.: InterVarsity Press, 1992), p. 63.

[8]F. A. Voigt, *Unto Caesar* (New York: Putnam, 1938), p. 267.

[9]Ibid., p. 57.

[10]Sue Lockwood-Summers, "An Evening Is a Terrible Thing to Waste," *Discipleship Journal*, November/December 1992, pp. 50-53. I have borrowed some good ideas from this article and recommend the article for other practical alternatives to TV watching for young families.

[11]Quoted by Terry Mattingly in "Spot the Lie," *Discipleship Journal,* November/December 1992, p. 51.

[12]Schultze, *Redeeming Television*, pp. 81-82.

[13]Lockwood-Summers, "An Evening Is a Terrible Thing to Waste," pp. 50-53. The question ideas were borrowed from this article.

[14]Lynette Friedrich Cofer and Robin Smith Jacobvitz, "The Loss of Moral Turf: Mass Media and Family Values," in *Rebuilding the Nest: A New Commitment to the American Family,* ed. David Blankenhorn, Steven Bayme and Jean Bethke Elshtain (Milwaukee, Wis.: Family Service America, 1990), p. 185.

[15]Hewlett, *When the Bough Breaks,* pp. 120-21.

[16]Ibid., pp. 121-24.

Chapter 12: Tempted to Forget the Discipline

[1]Jack O. Balswick and Judith K. Balswick, *The Family: A Christian Perspective on the Contemporary Home* (Grand Rapids, Mich.: Baker Book House, 1989), p. 99.

[2]Ibid., p. 101.

[3]Tom L. Eisenman, *Big People, Little People: A Course for Parents of Young Children* (Elgin, Ill.: David C. Cook, 1985), pp. 36-38. See also Merton P. Strommen and A. Irene Strommen, *Five Cries of Parents* (San Francisco: Harper & Row, 1985), pp. 145-46.

Chapter 13: Tempted to Give Up on God

[1]C. S. Lewis, *The Magician's Nephew* (New York: Macmillan, 1955), p. 142.